Josephus Nelson Larned

Talks about labour and concerning the evolution of justice between

the laborers and the capitalists

Josephus Nelson Larned

Talks about labour and concerning the evolution of justice between the laborers and the capitalists

ISBN/EAN: 9783337229542

Printed in Europe, USA, Canada, Australia, Japan

Cover: Foto ©Suzi / pixelio.de

More available books at **www.hansebooks.com**

TALKS ABOUT LABOR,

AND

CONCERNING THE EVOLUTION OF JUSTICE BETWEEN THE LABORERS AND THE CAPITALISTS.

BY

J. N. LARNED.

NEW YORK:

D. APPLETON AND COMPANY,

549 AND 551 BROADWAY.

1876.

INTRODUCTORY.

Nothing ambitious has been attempted in this little book. The writer has not undertaken to construct a social theory, nor to solve the grave problems which are involved in the relations existing between labor and capital, by any copyrighted or patented formula whatsoever. He has simply tried to investigate—for his own satisfaction in the first instance—the conditions under which the work of the world is done, and to do so with impartiality of feeling, as between the classes that contribute to it; to ascertain how far such conditions are conventional or arbitrary and how far they are naturally fixed; to discover, consequently, what readjustments appear practicable, and to learn, at the same time, what principles of justice are underlying the whole matter. He has aimed at nothing more, in a word, than to find the *direction* in which one may hopefully look for some more harmonious and more satisfactory conjunction of capital with labor than prevails in our present social state, by finding in what direction the rules of ethics and the laws of political economy tend together. That there must be such a coincidence between what is just and what is practicable — between material conditions and moral principles, in the evolution of society—he is persuaded firmly. If he has gained even a dim discernment of it, he has done all that he expected to do. Time alone can bring about the full discovery.

In submitting the meagre results of an earnest study of the subject, he has endeavored to present them as briefly and compactly as possible, only hoping to suggest to some other minds a mode of thought which they may be willing to pursue. He has also endeavored to present the argument of his view with fairness, and has adopted for that purpose—though with imperfect skill—the conversational form, in which both modifying and opposing considerations can be brought into a discussion most easily. This method of treating the subject has sometimes induced—in the opening chapters especially—an extremeness of statement on one side, which the counter-statement is trusted to correct. Taken alone, there are some statements of that kind, perhaps, which the writer would not wish to have accepted as sound teaching. If his view of the subject is considered at all, he would ask to have it considered as a whole.

J. N. L.

BUFFALO, *May*, 1876.

CONTENTS.

THIRD EVENING.

FOURTH EVENING.

FIFTH EVENING.

TALKS ABOUT LABOR.

FIRST EVENING.

THE judge (who is not a judge, by the way, but
only called so in familiar speech by some of us who
should like to see him on the bench) had lately
become my neighbor, living a few doors distant
on the same street. I knew that his home was
desolate and had lost its charm for him, because
the shadow of death which is darker than any
other had fallen on it not many months before.
So I proposed to him that he should drop in upon
me, for an evening smoke and an hour or two of
quiet talk, just as frequently as he might afford,
without keeping any account between us of visits
given or returned. He accepted the invitation

frankly, and came often during the winter to my
little study—as we style, with some complacency,
the modest chamber of our cottage in which I
smoke and read during idle hours at home.

It happened rather fortunately, I think, that
on the night when the judge came first I sat
with a newspaper in my hand, and had been reading in it the account of a certain wide-spread
" strike " among the workmen of some important
trade in the Eastern States. This led us into talk
upon a subject which I found had interested him
much, and on which he had been pondering, in
his characteristic way, with searching earnestness.

I had wheeled an easy-chair for him to the
front of the fire, which burned cheerfully in the
grate ; we had settled ourselves comfortably, with
full pipes, and surrounded ourselves satisfactorily
with that atmosphere of fragrant smoke in which
ideas float more lightly than they do in common
air. My wife, who likes the pleasant little room,
for all its smokiness—and none the less, perhaps,
because of that—sat opposite, half busy with some
bit of foolish sewing, as women like to be in their
leisure times, while my elder daughter Kate, in
the sitting-room just beyond, was entertaining a
young gentleman named John, whose frequent
visits, I began to see, had an object in them which
I could not altogether disapprove.

We had skirmished for a while in the region of small-talk, as people do until they have uncovered, on one side or the other, some ground on which they may engage in rational conversation, and at last, in a casual way, I made allusion to the matter of which I had been reading, and remarked that, even in this country of fewer hands than acres, the labor question, as it is called, or the question between capital and labor, is becoming a very serious one.

"I think," replied the judge, "that it has become already *the* question above all other questions in social importance, and that we have not another problem in the world to-day that is pressing upon us so sternly for an equitable solution as that one which is involved in the perpetual contention between capitalists and laborers."

I was surprised at the emphasis and earnestness with which he spoke on the subject, and, while I admitted the importance of this labor question, I doubted whether it could be held to take rank above all other questions, when we consider the many issues that remain in controversy among men, affecting their social state, both in morals and in government.

"Why," said he, "this labor question of to-day succeeds the slavery question of yesterday, inevitably, by the nature of things. Having determined that one man may not *own* the labor of

another man, how can we help going on to inquire
about and ascertain the just terms on which the
labor of one may be *used* by another? It is
plainly, to my mind, the sequent step—the next
proceeding in the inquisition of human rights,
which we are forced to enter upon, whether will-
ingly or not. Our civilization, as we call it, is,
more than anything else, an evolution of the sentiment of justice among men, and almost every
other fruit of civilization, in its moral aspect, is
incident to that or developed out of it. This results so from the kneading and moulding of men
into organic social masses—a process which tends
steadily to press out the savage egotism or selfism
which saturates the isolated human being. Now,
that sentiment of justice, or sensibility to injustice, in society, which has only to-day gathered
enlightenment enough to abhor a legal system
of servitude which it tolerated yesterday, cannot
have reached yet the end of its education in that
direction, but rather the beginning of new teachings that are larger and more exact. Just as surely
as it has recognized the hideous oppression of law
which made one man the master by ownership of
another, just so surely it is going to take cogni-
zance now of the oppression of those circumstances
in the social state which give to one an overmas-
tering power over his fellow.

"This movement of education among men to

a truer apprehension of justice and right, in place
of conventional notions which confuse the moral
sense, is not an eccentric one; it follows logical
paths to its several ends, and can be traced like
the construction of so many syllogisms in human
history. In fact, the slow judicial action of society,
sifting out rights from wrongs by clumsy methods
and tardy forms of procedure, and so establishing
equity between its members, is almost all there is
of history that is worth a serious studying. My
reading of the chronicles of our race is very much
to me as though I stood upon the threshold and
looked into some great judgment-hall, wherein
the painful formulation of an unwritten common
law of justice between man and man has been going on, since human history began, in passionate
litigation, in tedious argument, in hesitating but
irrevocable decisions. This solemn court of high
chancery sits always; knows no adjournment;
never suspends nor dismisses a cause. Its judges
and jury we cannot see, for they are of that
ghostly and changeful substance which has its
palpable but unseen forms, and which we call
'public opinion.' But the suitors, the clients, the
witnesses, the advocates, the attorneys, the bailiffs
—they throng the court. Whole nations fill its
wide galleries and its far-stretching corridors and
aisles, waiting for the verdicts which come so
slowly in. It is a merciless and an awful court;

its justice long delayed and very stern. Death
and terror are its frequent ministers; many times
its instruments have been pestilence and famine
and war, insurrection, revolution and massacre,
the dungeon, the scaffold and the stake. It has
issued its writs in blood, and executed them with
fire and sword. It wears out the lives of its lit-
igants with the weariness of its forms and the
heartlessness of its procedure. Generations die,
and son succeeds to son in the inheritance of every
wrong that is pleaded at its bar. But the verdict
of justice issues always at last; indisputably justice; inexorably the final and the absolute adju-
dication of right. At long intervals, of many
centuries sometimes, there is a pause and a stir in
the august chamber, and the voices of the criers
proclaim an old cause ended, the trial of a new
cause begun; the old cause settled forever and
ever, and sent out of court with the seal of an
everlasting judgment set upon it; the new cause
summoned to a hearing that will not rest until
the same irrevocable seal has been stamped upon
the decision of it. So, in times past, we have
heard the suit of the people against the king, the
suit of the commons against the lords, the suit of
conscience against the Church, cried into court
and cried out of court; and so, too, of late, not
least though last, we have heard the procla-
mation of justice declared in the long, long

suit of the slave and the serf against their masters.

"Now, I tell you, when the slave went out of court, a triumphant suitor, the laborer for hire came in and took his place; for when the great chancery court of civilization pronounced against the possession by one man of the labor of another through mastery, or force, or operation of law, it bound itself to go further in the matter and to investigate the equity of the terms under which one man, in any other way, may possess the fruits of another's labor; the equity, that is, of the division to be made between him who toils and him who possesses the tools and the materials with which and on which that toil is expended. The trial of this question is on. Its hearing has begun. It cannot be arrested by any injunction, nor by any change of venue, nor by any stopping of the ears nor shutting of the eyes. It will go on, and on, to the end, whether that be this century or the next one."

The judge is ordinarily a quiet man in his talk. I never had heard him speak in so fervid a temper and so oratorical a style before. I could see that his feelings had been deeply wrought upon by the subject, and I became curious to know what view of it had produced this effect on so dispassionate a mind.

My wife had dropped her sewing in her lap,

and her face wore something of a startled look.
"You have frightened me, almost," said she,
"with your vision of judgment; I never thought
of history in that way before. There is an awful
solemnity in the idea, and it does not seem to be
a fanciful one at all, but so real that I can almost
feel myself in the very presence of the inexorable
court."

"I have the same impression," was my re-
mark, "and the picture which the judge has drawn
is, without any doubt, as true as it is striking. But
I do not exactly see that the suit of the laborer
for a just partition of the products of labor is so
immediately sequent to that of the slave for his
freedom. It seems to me that the two questions
involved are so different, both in origin and in
principle, that the solution of one does not open
the way very much to a solution of the other.
The institution of slavery is a purely arbitrary one,
existing by virtue, only, of a determination on the
part of one body of men to oppress another body
of men, because they have the power to do so;
and nothing, therefore, but the willingness of society is needed at any time to break it up. But
the labor system, or the arrangement of the conditions under which labor for hire is performed,
seems to be rooted in the constitution of human
society, and the oppression or inequity that is incident to it appears to me to proceed out of circum-

stances over which society has little control, so far as we are yet able to perceive. I confess that I cannot understand how the sentiment of justice, which civilization is certainly developing, will have power to interfere with the operation of those inflexible laws, proceeding from a source of justice whose legislation we cannot comprehend, which have been imposed upon mankind and which govern, with a force stronger than human law can ever have, the whole organization of work in the world."

"Yes, I see," said the judge; "your perplexity is just that which one is placed in who examines this question under the lights only which our modern science of political economy throws upon it. A man who would be hopeful for humanity will not find much encouragement there. I used to be troubled very greatly until I began to see, as I see clearly now, that the labor question belongs but partly, not wholly, to political economy, and that more is assumed for that science than any true economist would claim, when we remit the question wholly to it for determination, as we are apt to think that we must do. I am profoundly a believer in political economy; that is to say, I am thoroughly, in the main, a disciple of those doctrines, political and social, which are grounded upon our systematic modern analysis of the creation and distribution of wealth. But political

economy is, or ought to be, strictly what may be
called a systematic science—a formulation, merely,
of facts as they exist.   It does not embrace, by
very far, even in the branches to which it relates,
the whole of social philosophy, because that extends to the searching out of causes and forces behind and superior to existing conditions and present facts. In the flush of enthusiasm produced
by the revelations that it has made to society within the last century, there is a tendency now to ele-
vate political economy, which has no right to be
anything else than a systematic, scientific formulation of certain existing social facts, into a social
philosophy, and that, I am sure, is a great mistake.

"However, this is not exactly to the point of
the question we are discussing.   Let me go back
to my proposition, that the labor question belongs
but partly to political economy, and cannot be re-
mitted for its solution altogether to the laws which
that science has determined.   It belongs in that
domain a little more, perhaps, but not much more,
after all, than did the slavery question, which, on
one side of it, was a stupendous economical question, and dealt with as such.   But we should have
waited very long for the forces which the political
economist is studying to bring about a solution of
it; longer, at least, than the civilized communities of mankind have been found willing to wait.
And so, in like manner, I believe, the simple jus-

tice of human society, as its education grows, is going to give every laborer his due share of what labor produces—more fairly at least than the majority have it now.

"You do not see, you say, that this labor question is immediately sequent to the question of slavery, and you view it as not belonging in the same category of human wrongs or inequities. But I am sure, if you consider a moment, you will concede that labor for hire, under the conditions which now exist, partakes, or may partake, very considerably, of the nature of slavery."

"Oh, no!" I exclaimed, "that is surely an exaggerated statement. There is, of course, an oppressive inequality, very often, in the relationship between the employer and the employed, but it has hardly a similitude to that terribly degrading subjugation of one man to another which slavery involves."

"Wait a moment," rejoined the judge. "Let me ask you to give a definition of slavery."

"I should say, in brief, that it is the forcible reduction of one man to a condition in which he is regarded and dealt with as the property of another."

"No; that is the form, only, which slavery wears when it accepts the name of slavery; it is not the essential fact in it. The real essence of slavery, as it seems to me, is the coercing of a man to yield the labor of his hands, or the service of his faculties, to the benefit of another man, without freedom or power to exact an equivalent return ; because, with some few exceptions, that is all which renders the enslaving of one man by another an object of desire. The motive of slaveholding, as a rule, we must look for in the gain, or the supposed gain, that is to be got by it. The essential fact of slavery, therefore, is this : that it places one man in possession of the labor of another under conditions which are compulsory on the latter, or which leave him no freedom or power to exact an equal return, and the statement of that fact seems to be the truest definition of slavery that can be given. What say you ? "

" I cannot dispute your definition."

" Well, then, we may fairly say that any condition in which a man is constrained to give the benefit of his labor to another, and exercises less than equal freedom in the arrangement of the terms of compensation upon which he does so, partakes more or less of the nature of slavery. Whatever difference there is must be of degree rather than of kind. Is not that true ? "

" We will concede that it is—at least until I have seen what conclusions it leads to."

" That is enough. Now let us see how far, in our present state of society, the conditions under which capital and labor operate together affect the freedom of the latter. To do so, we must start with ideas ·well defined. We must acquire a clear notion of what capital is and what its functions are, even though we have to go back to a few elementary statements, in order to set it with distinctness before our minds.

"In.the primitive state of mankind, as we conceive it, the human creature performs such little labor as he does without implements to help his hands, except the simplest weapons that can be used for killing, in the chase, and he directs his labor to immediate ends, which need no provision for time to be consumed in accomplishing them. He must hunt each day for that day's food, as the brutes do. The objects of his exertion are all objects of the moment; the means with which he exerts himself are just those with which Nature has furnished him, ready for the moment. When tools and implements begin to be made, either to expedite labor, or to make the doing of things possible which are not possible to the naked hands; or when labor begins to be applied to the producing of results which cannot be attained until to-morrow, or next week, or next month, or next year, that instant civilization begins, and that instant labor is placed under new conditions. Now, these new conditions, under which civilized labor is placed, are what we must particularly note and remember, for they are conditions on which it becomes as dependent as the new-born babe is dependent on the sustenance which others give it.

"When an implement is made, whether axe, or cart, or basket, or canoe, or rope, or whatever it may be, up to the latest most complicated machine, the man who makes it must have his immediate wants, of food, etc., in some way supplied to him while he is making it, either from a store of his own, or from a store provided by somebody else, who consents to supply his daily needs for the sake of a benefit from the implement when it is made. In the same way, when labor is applied to the producing of any remote or lasting, instead of an immediately beneficial result, as when a piece of soil is cleared and broken up for seed, and corn and roots are planted; or when herds and flocks are got together in pastures, for fattening and for breeding their increase; or when a road is made; or when a pack-peddler or a caravan or a ship is sent to carry things to some other place, to exchange for other things;—when any kind of work, in fact, is done, wherein the object of exertion is removed by some interval of time from the act of exertion, somebody must have saved or accumulated, out of the fruits of past labor, that which will supply the current wants of those whose labor directs itself to the remote result. So, too, when a division of labor has been brought about, and several men take each a distinct and special task for the benefit of all, becoming one a farmer, another a shoemaker, another a weaver of cloth, another a dresser of skins, and so on, there must be somewhere, in somebody's hands, a store from which they can draw while the exchanges between them are brought about, and while each one is partitioning to every other his contribution to the total wants of all. Without such a store for the interval of exchange, our division of labor, which is the material measure of civilization more than anything else, would be impossible.

"Now, all that, whatever it may be, which is so accumulated for these purposes, and so used, is capital. The nature and function of capital, therefore, we can best define by saying that it is everything, derived and accumulated from past labor, which enables present labor to be employed in any such way that the beneficial results from it have to be waited for.

"All this may seem trite, but we need to set it out freshly and distinctly before us in the discussion we have engaged in, because it defines the relationship between capital and labor. It brings us face to face with one tremendous fact: *that every kind of labor which does not immediately produce for the man who performs it the immediate satisfaction of an immediate want is absolutely dependent upon capital.* Now, put alongside of that a second grim fact, which no one will

dispute, viz.: *that this complex social state which
we call civilization has left no labor to be done by
any man that is not of that dependent kind,* or
next to none. Think of it! It cannot be realized
in an instant. We have to pause and reflect before we can fairly conceive the remoteness with
which almost every object for which we, any of
us, exert ourselves, is separated nowadays from
the exertion that we make, or the labor that we
perform, to attain it, no matter what may be the
particular division of human labor to which we
have assigned ourselves. We do something for
somebody in the next street, who does something
else for somebody else in the next town, who does
something else for somebody else in another State,
who does something else for somebody else in
New York, or in Boston, or in Chicago, or in New
Orleans, or in London, or in Paris, or in Calcutta,
who does something else for somebody else on an
Illinois farm, who grows the wheat that we make
our bread of, or on a South Carolina plantation, who
grows the cotton that is in our shirts, or on a Texas
pasture-range, who fattens the beef that we consume, or in an English factory, who weaves cloth
for our coats, or in a Chinese tea-garden, who
grows the herb which solaces our evening repast.
What man in the civilized world can trace the
intricate, devious, infinitely complicated way in
which the particular result of his particular labor

is raveled into a thousand threads, by our modern division of labor and the wonderful system of modern commercial exchange, to be woven in and out with millions of other threads, raveled and spun in the same way from the work of innumerable other hands, and so stretched hither and thither, all over the globe, to reach the ten thousand separate objects of want and desire for which he labors? No man *can* track, any longer, the work which he sends out from himself to a hundredth part of the results which it brings back to him. He cannot any longer, if he would, take things at first hands from Nature, by the immediate process of direct labor. Civilization has put everything at a certain remove, and capital, on every side of him, holds an intermediate agency.

"Here, then, entangled helplessly in the meshes of the vast network of this modern organization of labor and exchange, stands the man who has hands and brain, intelligence, strength, and will to work, according to the demand of Nature, for what he needs, but who stands empty-handed— with no accumulation of things hitherto produced —with no capital. What can he do? There are no wild creatures any more within his reach that he can hunt for food, or whose skins he can appropriate for clothing. There is not an animal that he can kill which is not the property of somebody—stamped with the right of possession by ac-

quirement or accumulation.   There is not a field
in which he can dig a root, or pluck an ear of corn,
or gather a handful of fruit, that is not hedged
with the same right.   There is nothing within his
reach to which he can apply his labor, to make it
productive for others and so exchangeable—not a
scrap of raw material, whether metal, or wood, or
stone, or even clay—that is not ticketed and la-
beled 'Hands off!'   The mark of appropriation,
the sign and seal of capital, are on everything
around him.   Except with the consent of the sov-
ereigns of this universal domain, if he so much as
attempts to apply his hands to any productive
work, he is a trespasser and a thief.   What can he
do?   Why, nothing, but helplessly cry out to those
who hold this environment of capital around him :
'Pray let me work! let me have something to work
with and work upon! land to cultivate, or wood
to cut, or iron to forge, or clay to mould and burn!
Give me a chance to produce something that is exchangeable for bread, with those who have bread.
Make your own terms with me—the best terms
that you can make with me and with my fellows
who, like me, have only capacity to work and desire to work, and who are utterly without the
means!   Take every advantage that you will of
the desperate pressure of our necessities !   Make us
bid against one another, until we bid ourselves
down to so small a share of the products of our la-

bor, expended upon your materials, with your implements, that it will barely keep our bodies and
our souls together; but let us work, and not
starve!'

"In God's name, my dear sir, is not the potent
possibility of oppression that exists here something
terrible? And when we have two classes of men,
with the possession of capital on one side and the
necessity to labor on the other, does not the relationship between them partake very considerably
of the nature of slavery?

"Mind you, I am not quarreling with this state
of things, nor denouncing it. I am only stating
the facts about it. I recognize it as being an inevitable incident of civilization up to the point
that we have reached; for, without having placed
ourselves under the conditions that produce it, we
could never have risen above barbarism. But I do
say that when civilization develops so frightful a
power in the hands of one part of mankind over
another part, it is the business of civilization to
find some way in which to counteract, or modify,
or nullify it, and it cannot have any other business
in hand that is half so imperative."

The judge had risen restlessly from his seat,
during the latter part of his speech, and was pac-
ing the room, in a singular state of excited feeling.
My daughter Kate and her young friend had stolen
into the study, attracted from their own topics by

2

the warmth and eloquence of ours. We had all
listened intently to the vehement declamation of
the judge, and, when he paused, there was a moment of thoughtful silence. I was moved a good
deal by what he had said, but not altogether convinced of the soundness of his view.

"Your statement," said I, after a little reflec-
tion, "your statement of the situation as between
labor and capital seems to me to be a theoretical·
and an extreme one. You represent the dependence of labor upon capital, but you do not take
into account the reciprocal dependence of capital
upon labor, which is just as rigorous a fact, and
which, if it be not quite equal to the other, goes
certainly very far toward neutralizing it. The
man of capital must have the help of the man of
labor to make his capital productive for him, just
as much as the laborer must have the help of the
capitalist to put him in the way of performing
productive work. The dependence is · mutual,
and there is a pressure of necessity on each side to
compel them to terms with one another, in the
matter of dividing whatever may be the joint product from what they severally contribute. You
leave this important fact out of the case, and present it one-sidedly, which is not fair nor true argument."

"Oh, no," cried the judge, "I do not forget the
dependence of capital upon labor—for its gains;

the necessity under which they both act together
in production; the self-interest which brings one
into coöperation with the other, when the two
exist apart, in separate hands. I do not forget,
and I have no wish to put out of sight nor to be-
little the facts that you refer to. I should have
come to them in a moment.

"The common interest which associates capital and labor together in production is a certain
fact, but we must take care to analyze it and see
its parts. I used to be deceived by it, and trusted
to it for a comfortable settlement of this whole
matter of justice to labor, until I happened one
day to think what a mighty difference there is between capital and labor in the abstract and the
capitalist and the laborer in the concrete. If you
place capital and labor together in the same hand
—let the same man, that is, be both laborer and
capitalist at once—there is then no possible issue
between them; their identification in interest and
their mutuality of dependence are complete; and
this is their natural state of union—the one which
we theoretically contemplate whenever we prove
to ourselves that there is natural justice in the relationship between them. But put them apart—
dissociate them so far as their personal representa-
tion is concerned, making the laborers one class
and the capitalists another class; what then? You
have put persons in the place of things, now, and

the situation is wholly changed. You are no
longer merely dealing with the inter-operative
functions of capital and labor in the abstract, but
you are dealing with them under the dominion of
concrete human motives and passions, human necessities and desires, and all the nice balance which
existed between them before is totally destroyed by
interference. The man of wealth, be it a greater or
less accumulation, is ordinarily covetous of more,
and so feels that it is for his interest to employ
what he possesses as capital, to produce an increase. He is commonly actuated in this by no
immediate necessity, but by a desire, or by prudential fore-calculations for the future. But the
man without wealth, who possesses nothing save
the ability to work—how enormously different are
the forces that act upon him! There are no alter-
natives in his case; no region of choice within
which he is free, except that narrow one which has
death on one side of it. He *must* employ his
labor productively in order to live. His interest
in the matter is the interest which a man has in
the preservation of his life, and of other lives that
are dear to him and dependent on him. When,
therefore, you bring these two together, to make
terms of copartnership with one another in the
business of production, you have love of gain to
urge the one and love of life to force the other.
Behind the one you have prudence, avarice and

many selfish desires; behind the other you have
hunger, misery, starvation, death. On one side
you have a powerful human motive ; on the other
side a desperate human necessity. Will you say
that the two contracting parties stand upon an
equal footing in their negotiation ? Will you expect to keep equity in the middle of such unequal
forces as these ? Will you trust your laws of political economy to secure justice to labor in such a
situation as this ? No, sir. It will not do. Those
are the theorists, in this matter, who talk of capital
and labor as though they were merely dead names
of things; as though they were nothing more than
the 'x' and the 'y' of a simple equation; as
though there were not a living, breathing, palpi-
tating humanity represented in them, whose needs
and misfortunes and passions complicate the problem. I am not the theorist, for I face the facts as
the world shows them to me, and they tell me
that it is an idle dream to look for fair dividends
to be made between capital and labor by simple
operation of the mutual interests which bring them
together."

"But, my dear judge," said I, " there certainly
is an extremeness in your statements. You will
not claim that the situation you have described is
actually and commonly the situation in which the
laborer makes his bargain with the capitalist.
How often does starvation really occur, even

among the poorest and most unfortunate of mankind, and how often does it appear so imminent
to any laborer that his fear of it will actually
dictate the wages to which he submits? You must
concede, I think, that the situation of 'desperate
necessity' is an exceptional and not the common
one, and that when it does occur, to any large extent, it is produced by causes of general misfor-
tune or calamity which have disturbed the whole
productive organization of society."

"Yes, but why is this so?" It is because here,
as in many other instances, the heart of man is
more generous than the social systems he has
framed. I think well of human nature, on the
whole, and I believe that kindness toward a fellow-
being is more in accordance with our nature than
cruelty; though it has to be developed, like every
other moral disposition in man, by intelligent perceptions. That is the ground on which I rest my
hope for humanity in the very matter that we are
speaking of. We eke out, now, a tyrannical and
heartless theoretic economy with practical charities
and generosities that make it tolerable. The
change to be brought about is this: that we must
reduce the generosity to a system, not of generosity, but of justice and right. According to the
theory of our wages system, the fortunate part of
mankind which has possessed itself, in one way
and another, of almost all the instruments and ma-

terials and adjuncts of productive labor, has a right
to compel the other part to perform work for just
that least and lowest share of the products of labor
which the competition of their bodily necessities
will force them to accept; but the practice of the
system is not often as heartless as the theory of it.
It seldom happens that the men of capital drive
the hardest and sharpest bargain that they might
with the men of labor. It seldom happens that
their cruel power is exercised to the terrible extreme which it might be carried to. It seldom
happens that the vast army of empty-handed men
and women, whose bread to-morrow depends upon
their chance to work to-day, are desperately driven
to bid each other down to quite such fragments
and crumbs of subsistence as they might be, if
there were no humanity nor generosity to leaven
the brutal selfishness of the theory of the system
to which they are subjected. Capital is all the
time giving something more of a share of the production which it controls to labor than it might
give, in somewhat higher wages than it might
pay; and, at the same time, a broad, grand organization of what we call philanthropy and benevo-
lence is overlaid upon the system of our social
economy, to mitigate its harshness and heartlessness. Contrary to their usual wont, men practise
in this matter of their responsibilities toward one
another better than their maxims prescribe, and I

feel assured, by a thousand signs, that the heart of humanity is very nearly right and ripe for something juster and fairer than the old institutions of labor. It is only waiting now for certain strong habits of view which it has acquired to be corrected by truer instincts and a larger enlightenment."

"As I understand you, then," said I, "your view is that capital holds over labor an oppressive advantage, which is not used, as a rule, to the full extent, but which it asserts, nevertheless, with too much sanction from the economical philosophy of our day, an unlimited right to use; and your demand is, that the claim of right to exercise so oppressive a power shall be condemned and vetoed by the just judgment of society."

"That is it. You have it exactly. And now —but here have I talked the whole evening away," cried the judge, looking at his watch, " and made you all dumb, very nearly, with my uncivil lecturing. I am ashamed of myself; but you threw me on a subject which runs away with me. I hope, ladies, you will not think that I am always such a rattle-tongued egotist as I have been to-night."

And so he went on with many laughing apologies until my wife had to put a stop to them, and compelled him to understand that the talk of the evening had interested her so greatly that she should be impatient for a continuation of it. Nor

would we any of us let him go until he had prom-
ised to come again, on the morrow, and resume
the topic where it had been left. On that promise
we bade him good-night, and, with hearts that had
grown much warmer toward him within the past
hour or two, we saw him walk slowly to his lonely
home.

SECOND EVENING.

ABOUT THE RIGHTS OF CAPITAL.

Might and Right in Society.—What morally belongs to Superior Endowments and Advantages.—The Point of Social Equilibrium.—Some Study of the Modes in which Wealth is acquired.—The Judge's Doctrine of Morals and his Doctrine of Justice.

FAITHFUL to the promise he had made, the judge came early the next night, and found us all waiting for him in the little room. My young friend John, whom I discovered to be a very sensible fellow indeed, had begged the privilege of being present again. He was much taken with the judge's talk, although the conservatism which is commonly incident to his time of life held him back, with more resistance than I could make, from the acceptance of the judge's views. The conservatism of young men, at a certain stage of experience, by-the-way, is a very curious thing; not strange at all, but curious. It is wholly contrary to the impulses of youth; but the contrariness, you see, is just as natural as the impulses

are, and perhaps a little more so. The boy is
pretty surely a radical ; all his philosophy of life
is full of romance, and enthusiasm, and credulity.
But the young man, having knocked his head and
stumbled with his feet a few times against the
hard realities of the world, becomes so distrustful
and afraid, very soon, of his enthusiasms, that he
tries hard to extinguish them, and pushes himself
with all his might to the opposite extreme of
thinking and feeling. Old notions of things, with
their wrinkles and their grayness, and with such
mouldiness even as they may have acquired, look
much wiser and more venerable than the sleek
upstart parvenues of doctrine which oppose them,
and he has not courage to refuse them a respectful
deference, whether they satisfy his judgment or
not. He fancies that they *must* be the true notions, and he is fearful and ashamed of any revolt
in himself against their claims, because he suspects
that it is proceeding out of some lingering boyish-
ness in him which he ought manfully to get rid
of. So he becomes resolutely conservative, in his
ambition to become manly, and mature, and dis-
creet. If selfish pursuits, of fortune or ambition,
gain possession of him then, as they are apt to do,
and he ceases to think much or care much for
things outside of his own objects in life, he is
more likely to retain his conservative attitude
thenceforward than to change it, simply as the

effect of a certain rheumatic rusting and stiffening
of his nature, rather than because of any constitutional bent of mind that he has. Now, my young
friend John was just at that stage of his life when
the fear of not being conservatively wise and prudent overcame pretty much all that was instinctive
and natural in his view of things. Being an ex-
cellent fellow, of industry, intelligence and a
steady character, he had risen to quite an important clerkship in one of the iron-working establishments of the city, with reasonable expectations of
a partnership in time; and in that situation, with
these prospects, of course he felt himself in a
measure responsible to society for the defending
and maintaining of its well-established arrangements and institutions. I was not surprised, therefore, to find him, although greatly pleased with
the judge, yet stoutly critical of his views, and
much disposed to be afraid of some hidden infec-
tion of communism, or other dangerous and de-
moralizing doctrine in them. I saw how it was
with the young gentleman, and knew that the talk
would do him good.

"Now," said the judge, after some greetings
and weather observations and the like, when we
had settled ourselves before the fire, "if we are
going to take up our old subject again, you must
not let me prose upon it as I did last night. We
must have more of a conversation and less of a

lecture this evening, if you will help to keep me from forgetting myself."

"But, you know," I suggested, "that we prefer to be listeners and questioners chiefly in this matter, because we have none of us reflected upon it as you have done, nor arrived at the convictions about it which you have. We are asking you to give us the results of your study and your thinking on the subject, and to show us the course of reasoning by which you have been led to your opinions."

"Yes," said my wife, "you must be generous, and not exact measure for measure."

"Well, well; we'll not be ceremonious nor disputatious about it," the judge cried; "but I shall endeavor not to play quite so oratorical a part as I certainly did last night. And now, where is our question? At what stage of argument did we drop it?"

I was ready to answer, but my wife proved too quick for me.

"Let me show you," said she, "how far a woman can be interested in these masculine topics, and how understandingly she may remember a discussion of them. You had shown that capital holds over labor a terribly oppressive advantage, which is dangerous and unjust to the latter, and which, although not fully exercised, is fully asserted as of right, and with a sanction from the economical philosophy of our time which ought not to be given to it."

"You have stated it with precision, madam, and admirably," said the judge. "I am sure that no one can wish to amend the statement. Are we agreed, then, to this point, or is there more to be questioned before we go further ?"

"I should like to ask a question," said Master John, blushing a little at his own boldness. "Is not the advantage which the capitalist holds, as against the laborer without capital, an advantage that belongs to him, by nature and by right, or by the intention of the Creator? Is it not, I mean, an advantage that inevitably accrues to him by reason of some superior capability that he is endowed with, and on account of which the possession of capital is gathered into his hands. It seems to me that, inasmuch as men are not created alike, it must be intended that each should have the benefit of whatever advantage is gained for him by his own peculiar faculties or his own peculiar character."

"This is an important question that you have raised," answered the judge, "and I am glad that you have brought it up. We must look into it. I should not like to dispute the right of a man to appropriate any benefit that legitimately accrues to him from the faculties or the forces which God has endowed him with. When I speak of equity between men I do not mean equality. There is no such thing as equality among men — except their equal right to an equal opportunity in the world, for doing according to their capabilities and according to whatever moral force is in them. I do contend for that equality, but for nothing more, and this is what I mean by equity. You would not say, I am sure, that *every* advantage which one man possesses over another, by reason of a superior natural endowment, can be equitably used to its full extent? For example, one is physically larger and stronger than another, so that, if he chooses to do so, and if society does in no way interfere, he may obtain mastery over his fellow by muscular superiority, and command him as a subject or a slave. Would you say, in that case, that the fortunately strong man has a right to all the advantage over his fellow which may accrue to him by reason of his muscular capabilities?"

"Certainly not," answered John; "we are not savages."

"And if one man, not being stronger than his fellow, but being more courageous and more energetic and aggressive, is still able to domineer over him and to place him in a position of dependence and servility, would you say that the advantage which he thus obtains belongs to him by nature and by right, and by the intention of the Creator, who made him a more aggressive creature than his neighbor ? "

"No, sir," said John, after a little hesitation, "I should not."

"Once again, then : if one man, without being stronger or more courageous than his fellow, is more intelligent and inventive, and succeeds, therefore, in contriving weapons which his neighbor cannot resist, and in protecting himself with armor which his neighbor cannot penetrate, so that he is able to override his neighbor, as the mediæval knight did the peasant, and to do as he will with him—would you say that the advantage which accrues in this way from a superior capability belongs to its possessor by right, and that society or social opinion has no business to interfere with it ? "

"I do not think that I should say so," replied John, with much frankness; "but these examples that you suggest all look to the exercise of a tyrannical brute force, which civilized society, of course, cannot tolerate."

"Yes, but why ? I have adduced three instances in which a man may be given the utmost results of an advantage over his fellow-men obtained by the possession of a superior capability. In our first example the advantage is a physical one—that of muscular strength ; in the second it is a moral one—that of courage and energy ; in the third it is an intellectual one—that of knowledge and invention. The three sides of human nature are represented in these three examples, and you admit, therefore, that there may accrue advantages to a man from every kind of capability that the human being can possess which he has no right to enjoy, or which society cannot afford to concede to him. Now, what is the distinction to be drawn between advantages which rightfully belong to the man who possesses a superior capability and those which do not rightfully belong to him?"

My young friend John could not answer.

"Perhaps we can find out," continued the judge, "by a little more questioning. If the stronger man has no right to subjugate his fellow-man, by the superior strength that he possesses, he has a right, has he not, to the larger product of the more efficient labor which his superior strength enables him to perform?"

"Undoubtedly."

"And the more energetic and enterprising man has a right to the enjoyment of what he achieves by his superior activity and resolution, in fair competition with his neighbors?"

"Certainly."

"And the intelligent man who makes his knowledge or his inventive faculty helpful to him in his work, has a right to the benefit, has he not?"

" Assuredly."

"It seems, therefore, that according to our sense of right, there are some advantages which the man who is more capable, in any wise, than his fellow, may justly take from his fortunate endowment, and some which he may not take with justice. Consequently the mere fact that such an advantage is placed within his power by the Creator who endowed him, does not prove, I should say, that it belongs to him to appropriate at will."

" That is true, I must admit," said John.

" Just what does belong to him by right, and what does not," continued the judge, " may not be so easy to determine exactly. We may safely say, however, that a man has a right to the benefit of every advantage, accruing to him from any kind of superior capability, which is not a disadvantage to his fellow-man, or which is not exercised at the expense of his fellow."

We all assented.

" I think, too, that the converse of this proposition is equally true, and that no man has a just right to any use of any advantage in this world which takes aught from the advantages or opportunities of any other man. But this may raise nice questions in some cases, and I will not start them by asserting it. The wings of genius would sometimes be clipped if that were made the rule. It is enough for our present inquiry that we settle

so much as we have settled; that might of any
kind does not make right, whether the potentiality
in question be that of strength, or courage, or cunning, of industry, or economy, or enterprise. The
great fact to be recognized—the fact essential to
human civilization—is this: that every gift to a
man, in his body, or in his mind, or in his soul, is
an obligation as well as a gift; that he holds it for
his fellows as well as for himself, and that each
one is so far his brother's keeper that he is bound
to take care, at least, that his brother be not
harmed nor hindered by him."

" That is good doctrine," exclaimed my wife.

"It is the philosophy of Christianity on its human side," said I.

"You are right," confessed John, " and I see
that the point which I raised against your argument of last night was not well considered."

"It is not necessary, then," said the judge,
" to go further into this part of our subject. But
I think it may do us some good, nevertheless, to
consider how it is, under what circumstances and
through what causes, of superior capability or
otherwise, that the capital accumulated by human
industry comes to be gathered, for the most part,
into the hands of a comparatively few men, while
the rest hold none at all or very little. When we
speak of capitalists, we usually refer to the rich
men of the community, whose wealth is, more or

less, employed productively, either by themselves
or by others to whom they lend it. We must remember, however, that the term capitalists includes
a great multitude besides, who are not to be considered rich men, but who possess some surplus,
more or less, from a few dollars to a few thousands
of dollars in efficient value, which they employ in
connection with their own labor, as tradesmen, as
manufacturers, as farmers, as mechanics, etc. We
must put them all, of every degree together, to
constitute what can properly be called the capitalist class, as distinguished from the non-capitalist
laboring class. Let us do so, imaginatively, and
survey the congregation which has the Rothschilds
and the Astors at one extreme, while at the other
extreme are the humble blacksmiths and shoe-
makers, whose little capital is just that which will
furnish them with shops and tools, and which will
buy the material that goes into a job of work in
advance of its being paid for, besides furnishing
food while the work is being done. Taking them
all together, I wish to consider a moment the
various ways in which they have severally become
possessed of their capital.

"First of all, there is the capital that has been
accumulated in the hands that hold it by industry
and economy; by hard work, producing as much
as possible, and by saving or unwasteful habits,
consuming as little as may be. Most of the smaller

capitals are of this description, and they are held by the highest kind of right, because they represent a surplus of actual production, retained by and belonging to the men whose exertion produced it. The largest rights that can be claimed for capital must be conceded to those who hold it by this tenure.

"Next, there is the capital that accrues to those whom we call men of superior business capability, by the operation, on a large scale, of the faculty which they possess of organizing and directing productive industry; of giving the highest efficiency to it in any department, and of practically perfecting the systematic economy of labor and its exchanges. Also that which accrues to those who improve the arts of industry by discovery and invention, and to those who extend its fields and render its economical relationships more intimate, by enterprising and sagacious undertakings. The capital which accrues in these ways to men of faculty and energy, under the just limitations that we have settled upon, is as honestly gotten and as rightfully held as the other.

"After this, there comes the capital that is acquired in the hands of those who possess it by what we call successful speculation; by shrewdly or sagaciously taking advantage of opportunities in trade which are produced by circumstances outside of themselves, and relative to which they have no agency, except that of looking out for them and detecting them. The capital thus gotten together seems to me to be of very dubious tenure and the rights morally attaching to it very doubtful. In the hands that hold it, it does not, either directly or indirectly, represent production, but acquisition. It is acquired, generally speaking, at the expense of others. While the faculties that belong to the thrifty mechanic, the energetic manufacturer, the ingenious inventor and the sagacious projector, are all useful and beneficial to society, the faculty of the speculator is not so at all, but only beneficial to himself. It enables him to gain possession of that which he has in no way helped to produce. It is a kind of predatory talent, and deserves, I think, very little admiration or respect. In many cases the exercise of it is not morally to be distinguished from adroit theft; in some cases it is meaner and more despicable than theft. The mode of robbery which the footpad and the burglar pursue is an honorable and an honest one compared with the villainous stratagems that are contrived by the gambling speculators of the stock-market and the grain-market. Though society tolerates the robbery that is committed by a speculative 'corner' and condemns robbery committed on the highway with a pistol, the first is the meaner theft of the two, and the more detestable. Its indirectness has confused the moral notions of mankind; but some day, I trust, we shall have clearer ideas about it prevailing in society.

"By another kind of acquisition, capital is deposited, so to speak, in the hands of those who become possessors of it, without any agency at all on their own part, either honest or dishonest, either prudential, or sagacious, or crafty. They are only passive recipients of what fortune, or good luck, as we call it, has thrown upon them. Of such capitalists there are two classes: The first is made up of those who inherit an accumulation of wealth. Their own exertions have had nothing to do with the acquisition of it. It has passed into their possession either by gift, or under ordinances of society which are wholly founded upon considerations of expediency. There is no such thing as a natural right of inheritance, touching any kind of desirable possession, whether it be a house, or a public office, or an honorable title. There is no inherent reason of justice which determines that a son shall become possessed of the wealth which his father has acquired, when the father dies. Still less is there any naturally just reason which determines that the wealth accumulated by a man during his life shall pass, when he dies, to the living person of nearest kinship to him in blood, whatever the remove may be. The law which dictates this transmission of property by inheritance is one

purely of human institution. Thus far in the
development of society, men have agreed, and with
undoubted prudence, that such an arrangement is
practically the best, for the preservation of social
order and for the conservation of social stability;
but at some future time the agreement in society
about the disposition to be made by law, when a
man dies, of such wealth as his exertions have
accumulated, may be very different, perhaps. It
certainly can be so with perfect justice, because
the arrangement, as I conceive, is one to be governed entirely by the interest and well-being of
society, as determined, at any time, by its condition or by the general judgment of its members.
If the support and education of children until they
arrive at a mature age, and the decent support of
a surviving widow, are provided for out of the
estate of a deceased husband and father—who is
the responsible protector of these dependents
while they are dependent necessarily, and not
longer—natural justice would seem to be fully
satisfied. At all events, even if the possessor of
inherited wealth be fully entitled to the luxury
of living and to the exemption from necessitated
labor which it affords him, there cannot conceiv-
ably accrue to him from it such rights as *must*
attach to the accidental possession if we concede,
sir, that the advantages which the man with capital holds over the man without capital *are* rights.

The question here is an important one, because a very large part of the capital accumulated in the world is held by this tenure of inheritance.

" Much the same may be said concerning the second class of those who become possessors of capital with no more, or hardly more, than a passive agency on their own part in the acquisition of it. This class, which is a large one, is made up of men who, possessing by actual acquisition some property of small value originally, have a great accretion of exchangeable value added to it, through the incidental effect of labor performed by others around them, or through an increase of neighboring population, or through some such cause foreign to their own exertions. The property in which such an accretion of exchangeable value occurs is usually property in land, or real estate, as we call it. A man becomes possessed, for example, of a piece of land, to which no other value attaches, in the first instance, than the productive value of its soil. But a city grows up around it, and industry and commerce are so concentrated about the spot in which this piece of land happens to lie that mere space, in square inches and square feet, acquires just there a great artificial value, relatively to the value of other things. By selling his land, or by taking rent for its use, the man becomes rich—becomes largely possessed of capital, if he chooses to employ it as such—without

.3

any exertion of his own, and oftentimes without
any fore-calculation even of the causes which operated to give value to his land. Now, I am not
going to raise a question as to his right to the
wealth which accrues to him in this way, although
it is very much of a question whether private
property in land should exist at all. I certainly
cannot, for myself, satisfactorily refute those cogent
arguments which sustain the doctrine that the soil
and surface of the earth are the common property
of its inhabitants; that individuals can rightfully
appropriate nothing more than the use of such
portions of soil and superficial space as they do
use, and can only do that with the consent and
under the control of the community and state in
which they live. In this view, the only right of
property which a man can have in land is that
relating to the value which he creates in it, or
upon it, by his own productive exertions; for all
such fixed improvements as he makes, by clearing,
by draining, by fertilizing, by inclosing, by erect-
ing buildings, etc., are as certainly his own as the
movable things which his labor has produced;
but any other 'real estate' than that belongs very
doubtfully to any individual. However, we need
not, as I said, raise the question now. The only
point which I wish to make is this: that when
wealth is gathered, as so much of the wealth of
the world is gathered, into the hands that hold it at

any given time, by mere accretion of relative value
in some piece of land which a man has acciden-
tally acquired, and when that accretion is inci-
dentally brought about by the operation of human
energies which the man himself has very likely
contributed nothing to, it cannot be, in such cases,
that the possessor of this wealth becomes endowed
by it with any such rights as our young friend
proposes to concede to the capitalist, and which
are practically conceded to him in the politico-
economical philosophy of the present day. It cannot be so, because we cannot possibly reconcile
such an idea with our sense of justice.

"There is only one more way in which capital
is acquired that I must notice. It is the method
of outright, recognized dishonesty; by cheating
and overreaching, by adulteration and deception,
by bribery and corruption; by practising upon
the ignorance, the credulity, or the carelessness of
men, and by all the many knavish tricks which
evade or defy our criminal laws, and which the
technicalities of law often make an actual cover
for. It is quite unnecessary to ask what just
rights belong to the possessors of capital acquired
in these ways, as attaching to the advantages which
they derive from it; because, of course, they have
none. It is obvious that their possession of what
they hold is due merely to the toleration by society of a recognized injustice which it is impotent

as yet to prevent. But it would be sickening, I am afraid, to inquire how much of the existing capital of the world is held in the hands of men who have acquired it by sinister means of this sort.

" We have, then, if I have classified correctly, five generically differing processes by which all existing capital has accumulated, or become aggregated, in the hands of its present possessors. Broadly generalizing, I think that all the wealth or capital existing (and for the moment we may as well draw no distinction between wealth and capital) is embraced in these five categories :

" 1. Capital which is the residue that unwasteful consumption leaves to industrious labor, in the hands of those who have performed the labor. This includes the surplus earnings of all usefully-applied labor ; not only that which is directly productive, but that which the actual producers need or desire to have performed for them. It includes, therefore, the labor of physicians, surgeons, lawyers, clergymen, artists, literary men, and the like.

" 2. Capital which accrues to those who have the faculty to organize and direct with efficiency the productive labor of others ; or the faculty to make large, economical combinations in the exchanging of the products of labor between different parts of the world ; or the ingenious faculty which improves the implements and processes of productive industry ; or the enterprising, sagacious faculty that conceives and carries out great public works, which result in wider and more intimate relations between the diverse industries of the world.

" 3. Capital that is gotten into possession by what we call speculation, which is either mere gambling or a shrewd catching of opportunities in trade, produced very often by public calamities, or by disturbances of industry and commerce that are adverse to the public weal.

" 4. Capital that is received by inheritance, or otherwise passively acquired by its possessors, without any agency, or a very small agency, of their own, in the acquisition of it.

" 5. Capital that is acquired by actual, unquestionable fraud.

" We may generalize further, perhaps, and reduce our five categories to two, dividing all wealth, and therefore all capital, into two parts, separated by one most essential distinction :

" 1. Capital held by those who have contributed more or less to the creation of it.

" 2. Capital held by those who have contributed little or nothing to the creation of it.

" Now is it consistent, let me ask, with your notion of justice, as between men, that capital, which is the product of human industry, should be held in possession by men who have performed none of the labor that produced it, nor any such

labor as assists, or educates, or inspires, or grati-
fies the wants of those who produced it, unless it
is possessed by gift?"

This question was addressed to Master John,
who promptly answered: "No, sir, it is not. If
strict justice were to prevail, I am sure there could
be no such thing possible as the possessing of
wealth or capital without having created it, unless it had been conferred by gift, or by some
equitable exchange with those who did create it.
But is such final justice possible?"

"Ah, that is a later question," said the judge;
"we are discussing principles now. At least in our
accepted beliefs we should aim, I think, to sustain
that which is absolutely right and true, without regard to what may or may not seem to be practicable
for the moment. You do not dispute the proposition that capital ought in strict justice to belong,
as a prevailing rule at least, to those who have
contributed to the producing of it, or who have
contributed in some way to the satisfying of the
wants of its producers?"

"No; I should say that the proposition cannot be reasonably disputed."

"And it appears to be the fact, does it not,
that a very large part of the wealth or capital so
far accumulated in the world has passed, by one
means and another, into the possession of men
who can show no such title to the possession, or

who can show the right for a small portion only
of what they hold ? "

" Yes."

" Do you think it is an exaggeration to say
that one-third of all the wealth now existing has
been gathered into the hands of its present holders by inheritance, by passive accretion of value
(relatively or exchangeably), by speculation, by
gambling, and by various kinds of. fraud ? "

" No ; I am afraid that more than that proportion of the whole, rather than less, would be
found, on a strict inquiry, to fall within your. categories of questionably-acquired capital."

" Then," said the judge, " the inequity of the ·
distribution of wealth is surely a very serious
matter ; and if there is any upward movement of
development in humanity, as I, for one, firmly
believe, then there must be a discoverable tendency in society toward the correction of this inequity, by the operation of social forces and influences which have a just direction. If we only
investigate as political economy guides us, we
shall make no such discovery, because the political economist takes account of no motive in human action except self-interest or selfishness. Scientifically he has no right to take account of any
other motive, because his business is simply to investigate correlatively the conditions under which
the exertions of men are applied to produce the

satisfaction of their wants and desires, and he has gone to the proper limit of his science when he has formulated into laws the operation of this one impulse, from self, which acts in all human industry. I have no quarrel to make with political economy, as I said last night. I only contend that there is a larger social philosophy—an ethical economy, so to speak—which embraces political economy and extends far outside of it, and into the wider domain of which we have got to carry such questions as this. When I look there, it seems to me that I can see a gradual evolution of what I would call moral intelligence in the civilized world, which tends, though very slowly, to modify the great impelling force of selfishness in all directions, and even, therefore, in the acquisition of wealth. It is certainly a very slow evolution, and the fact that it is so does not discourage my faith.

" I do not believe, you know, in ignorant morality. Happily for the world, there is, oftentimes, among men, without the least rationality of conscience, a certain negative rectitude of conduct which bears some resemblance to virtue, but which is not of the true quality of virtue at all. It is altogether a negative thing. It is right conduct because it is not wrong conduct, that is all. It may come of feebleness, it may come of simpleness, it may come of mere dull, plastic obedience to some guiding religious authority; but it does not come of any vital moral force, and is of no account whatever in an estimate of the moral condition of mankind. To do right from an understanding of right is, in my view, the only genuine virtue. ·

"Truth and right are always coincident with pure reason, and every notion of right and wrong that we have, as I conceive, is derived from the reasoning intelligence, which God gave us for our enlightenment in this way as in all other ways. But the concepts out of which these moral notions are logically formed come from outside the region of sensual discovery, so that the reason is not helped by the senses to recognize their logical relationships, as it is helped in the whole domain of scientific knowledge. It necessarily works, therefore, toward the apprehension of moral truth with far greater slowness and difficulty than toward the apprehension of that which is sensibly phenomenal; it needs, too, a far longer exercise and culture to prepare it for as ready and clear a comprehension of such truth. Who can wonder, then, if what we call the intellectual development of mankind is far in advance of its moral development? It could not be otherwise. The necessary difference is so great that we can see nothing proportionate in it; and yet there is, unquestionably, a certain ratio, always, between, for example,

the scientific knowledge and the moral development of the human race. The easier objective
work of the human reason is its training for the
harder subjective work which it is equally ap-
pointed to do, and the evolution of moral intelligence by the latter keeps pace with the evolution
of scientific, artistic, and political intelligence by
the former, though lingeringly and far behind.
No doubt the separation is an increasing one, and
that fact is deceptive to us; but it is like the race-
running of the tortoise and the hare—the distance
between them augments while both advance, and
even though there may be some constant and proportionate acceleration of the progress of both.

"There is this order, as I believe, in the development of humanity : 1. Toward objective or sen-
suous intelligence ; 2. Toward subjective or moral
intelligence ; 3. Toward the disciplining of the
animal man to act in accord with his intelligence.
The first of these will always be far in advance of
the second ; the second always in advance of the
third ; and yet the first and the second contribute
steadily to the last, in which their whole divine
purpose would seem to be consummated.

" Our faith in the moral progress of man is apt
to be foolishly discouraged because his conduct
continues to be so far in opposition to what he
does apprehend of right and wrong. Yet there is
that same perversity of conduct, opposed to knowl-

edge, even where the strongest persuasions of mere animal selfishness coöperate with the understanding to restrain it. In the care of our bodies, for example, we act just as far in contradiction of what we know of the facts of physiology, of hygiene, and of sanitary science, as we act in contravention of what we understand to be right and wrong in our moral relationships. The perversity of conduct signifies no more in one case than in the other. In every case it only signifies the imperfect training of the animal and the volitional parts of man to obey the reasoning force in him, which is the sovereign force, nevertheless, and which is surely destined, in the Divine plan, to dominate completely at last. That such training goes steadily on, however slowly, and that men do act, in all ways, a little more according to what they know, however far their doing may still fall behind their knowing, I am not able, for one, to doubt."

"But," I interposed at this point, "how does your theory tally with the facts of human history? Do we not find the fundamental ideas of right and wrong as well developed and as well defined in the earlier historic stages of civilization as we do now?"

"Oh, yes," replied the judge, "the primitive, fundamental ideas of right and wrong are among the simplest, and therefore among the earliest ideas that man acquires. Some of them are so simple and so primitive that they are almost like the axioms of mathematical science, which we call self-evident propositions, because they contain in the very statement of them all the reasoning that enters into their construction. The difficulty to the human intelligence is not in laying hold of these first principles of right, but in combining and in applying them, as rules of conduct, under varying circumstances and conditions, and in varying situations, to varying human relationships. While it easily learns to shift its application of fundamental laws in science, or art, or politics, it is readily confused and perpetually loses its bearings, so to speak, in carrying a moral truth from one group of relationships to another. The same thing is true of all the subjective movements of the human intellect—in all ratiocinative operations where it passes outside of tangible things, and away from the coöperation of the serviceable senses of the human body. I am speaking, of course, of the average human mind, as represented by the mass of men and women, and I do not take account of the exceptional few who are given to be tutors of the many. Take an example from our present topic: the simple idea of the right of property is one of the fundamental ideas of right, and constructed very simply, out of little more than the ego and non-ego, or self-consciousness for its first element and the cognition of another self for its second. I have no doubt that the moral law, ' Thou shalt not steal,' was apprehended by the more advanced tribes of men long before its deliverance on Mount Sinai. But those who could see it to be a law of right conduct between themselves and their familiar neighbors, whom they were habituated to look upon as fellow-men, fellow-citizens, fellow-members, that is, of their own tribe and nation, could not carry it to its universal application without becoming confused and lost. Consequently, in the very community where theft, or the seizure of another's goods, had become a recognized wrong, as between its own members, we continually find piracy and predatory warfare upon alien or separated communities to be fully approved and never thought of as conduct possessing the same wrongful nature. The simple explanation of this repeated anomaly in human history—an anomaly which is still repeated, to no small extent, even within our civilized regions—is, that the moral intelligence of the average man requires long culture before it is able to give universal application even to the oldest maxims of right, and is not confused and betrayed by habitual notions of nationality, or race, or sect, or class, or by the simplest variations of circumstance. If you were to contrive to-day some ingenious new way of gaining possession of the property of another without the owner's consent, society at large would be a long time, I venture to say, in getting it catalogued in the list of recognized dishonesties. To the majority of men, a variation from the simplest form of stealing does actually disguise or obscure the fact that it is stealing. The same slow awkwardness appears in the handling of every other moral truth by the average human intellect, no matter how fully acquired the truth may be in its primitive nakedness. When you take this human intelligence of ours away from the region of sensible objects, where it can measure and mark its bearings, by visual reference to every-day objects and every-day phenomena, as the surveyor does when he is running a right line, it is easily led astray ; and I do not wonder when I find it so. It is quite according to Nature, I think, that the human reason should need much culture before it can deal with subjective ideas as easily as it deals with objective ideas, and therefore I expect the objective advancement of the intelligence of mankind to be far in advance of its subjective or moral development, while I am very sure, nevertheless, that the one is everlastingly a contribution to the other.

"But very likely you do not see what bearing all this moral philosophy has on our present question ?"

I admitted that I did not see the bearing exactly.

" Well," said the judge, " I have gone into it
a little because this doctrine of morals is at the
bottom of my whole social philosophy. It is the
justification I have to offer for my faith in an ultimate determination of equity between the capitalist and the laborer, which political economy
does not promise ; and also because it is necessarily preliminary to two or three questions that I
wish to ask before we drop our subject to-night.
I wish to ask you if you think that downright,
direct robbery is as rife in this generation as it was
last century, within what we call the civilized communities ? In other words, if professional rob-
bers, such as highwaymen, brigands, pirates, burg-
lars, etc., who plunder their fellow-men without
any disguise, are as numerous as they were ? "

After a little consideration we all said, " No."

" Some progress has been made, then," said
the judge, " in diminishing theft of the undis-
guised sort, at least. Now, what has been the
agent ? Do you think that law has done it, by
increased vigor and efficiency ? You must remember that the law was terribly merciless a hundred years ago in its dealing with these crimes
against property ; terribly merciless and savagely
vigilant. It hanged men and women for trivial
thefts, and kept its executioners busy. Since our
century began, the tendency of the law has been
all the time toward a milder spirit, with not much

increase, that I can see, in the energy of its police. It is true that gas-lighting and newspapers
and the telegraph have multiplied the eyes, ears,
and arms of the law to a wonderful extent; but
still, when all reasonable credit is given to these
modern agencies in the police system of society,
do you think that the great diminution which has
taken place in common theft and violent robbery
can be attributed altogether to an augmentation
of force in government and law?"

"No," said I, "unless the law gains in efficiency by the lessening of its rigor."

"But that cannot be, my dear sir, unless there
is some other restraining force in coöperation with
the law, which the law gives room to, by a wise
retirement of its own energies. Now, that is
just the point I was coming to. There is such a
morally restraining force, which slowly evolves
itself in society, and which, as it is generated, becomes more powerful than law. It is public sentiment, as we call it, or the prevailing enlightenment of a given community at a given time, with
reference to the applications of a given principle
of right. This moral intelligence, first gathering
into forcefulness among the few, percolates down-
ward with sure slowness into the duller mass,
and works a gradual change in the general disposition of society toward particular forms of wrong-
doing. Within the past century it has operated to

render all kinds of simple stealing and violent robbery more disgraceful than they used to be; that is to say, it has placed the human mind, in civilized countries, more generally in an attitude of contempt toward them; and the contempt of mankind is more terrible to the average human being than scaffolds or prisons are. A certain admiration of heroism used to be conceded, not more than a generation ago, to the boldness of the footpad and the daring of the burglar—to the Jack Sheppards, the Dick Turpins, and the Morrills of that time—which all the audacity of the 'James Brothers' and the 'Younger Brothers' and their sort in our day cannot inspire. The romance of these crimes is utterly gone. The common moral intelligence of mankind has been developed far enough to recognize the despicable villainy of a thief and robber, no matter what qualities of courage or coolness, dexterity, invention, or enterprise, may surround and color it. Toward all modes of outright theft and robbery the public sentiment of society has become condemnatory and contemptuous, as it never was before; and that, more than all other reasons, accounts to me for the diminished prevalence and audacity of these crimes.

"In the same way, ordinary gambling, which was the fashion of society a hundred years ago, and not merely tolerated but approved, has now become disreputable, and is driven, for the most part, into shame-faced hiding. So, too, has dueling been suppressed, in all the better civilized countries, not by law, but by public sentiment, or by what I call a moral intelligence, which has become so far·advanced that no sham code of honor, or pride of physical courage, and no specious differences of manner and circumstance in the deed, can blind it any longer to the murder that is done when one human being kills another with deliberation and intent.

"These facts, and many more of the same kind which I might adduce, are very significant to me. They teach us, I think, in what way to look for the moral improvement of society and what to expect as an evolution of justice and right. They teach me to believe that there *is* being developed, in the common crowd of human beings, a better state of moral intelligence, which slowly tends to the detection of theft in all its disguises, one by one, and which shall brand in time the man who steals his neighbor's goods by cheating in trade, or by overreaching, or chicanery, or fraud, or by dishonest cunning of any kind, as much as the man who steals by picking a pocket or picking a lock ; and which shall pronounce, too, against gambling with stocks or with commodities of the market as strongly as against gambling with dice and cards. But, if the gradual clearing of this moral intelli-

gence tends that way, toward the recognizing
and enforcing of rules of honesty in the conduct
of men, it tends still more obviously, I think,
toward the recognition and enforcement of rules
of justice between them. For it is plain to me
that the generalizing of such laws of justice as do
not concern property alone has made greater progress of late than the generalizing of the law of
honesty, or of property-rights, although it is the
greater generalization of the two, and really com-
prehends the other, because honesty is but one
particular of justice, and nothing more. With
reference, therefore, to all the modes in which
wealth becomes partitioned among men, I firmly believe that we are tending, in a slow, sure
way, toward equity, though not, as we must care-
fully remember, toward equality."

"You are right, judge," cried I; "you are
right. I am convinced that your hopeful doctrine
of justice is founded well, in reason and upon fact,
although the forces to which you intrust your faith
act so feebly and so slowly that one needs a pro-
found philosophy to keep fast his faithfulness to
them. I am only impatient now to learn how,
and with what clearness, you see a way for the
working of these just forces through the prodigious
difficulties that environ them."

"We have not come to the difficulties yet,"
said the judge. "We must determine first what

ought to be the adjustment made between capital and labor, or what would be if the terms of their copartnership in production were settled on pure principles of justice and right. Then will be the time to consider such obstacles as our doctrine of justice may have to encounter in the way of its realization. We cannot reach that point to-night, for it is late already, and we' had better adjourn the discussion to another evening."

" Let it be soon," exclaimed my wife, " for I want to know the difficulties. I feel eager for the prevailing of this doctrine of justice, and am anxious to know how long the world may have to wait for it."

" It shall be an early evening, then," the judge replied, as he rose, and we fixed our time before he took his leave.

THIRD EVENING.

The Comparative Quality of "Business" Faculties, and the Excessive Premium put upon them.—The Judge's Coöperative Theory. — Trades-Unions and Labor-Strikes. — The Preaching and Teaching that need to go together.

"Now, judge," said I, when we had reassembled, on the third evening, and after we had exchanged a bit or two of gossip, by way of relish, "I shall assume to be the presiding officer of this august assemblage, and call to order. We will take up the unfinished business of our last sitting, and the question, I believe, is on the motion of the gentleman from the iron district, that we declare those advantages which the man of capital holds over the man without capital to be rights which belong to him, and which he may fully exercise as it pleaseth him to do. Are you ready for the question?"

"But," interposed John, "if I may be permitted to correct the speaker, I think it will be remembered that I withdrew that motion, as you

see fit to call it, after listening to the argument of
the distinguished gentleman on my right."

"Never mind," said the judge, "I shall be
glad to have the question considered as being still
before the house, because there are some things
more to be noticed before we dismiss it. I do
like, however, in a discussion such as this, to be
sure that we are keeping step with each other, and
that we understand one another at every point in
our discourse. I propose, therefore, that we just
glance back for a moment, over the ground we
have traversed, and see whether we entirely agree
in our conclusions."

We showed our assent, and the judge went on:

"In order to be exact, I have written a little
series of propositions, which are the summing up,
in my view, of the conclusions established in our
talk thus far. They are these:

"1. No productive work of any kind can now
be done, in most parts of the world, without the
help of capital.

"2. The men who have acquired no capital
are compelled to solicit that help by the most inexorable of all human necessities—the necessity
for bread, clothing, and shelter ; while the men
who have acquired capital are impelled on their
part to yield it by nothing more strenuous, so
far as circumstances go, than a selfish motive—
the desire for gain.

" 3. The relationship between these two classes, therefore, if nothing intervenes, is one of independence on the side of capital and of dependence on the side of labor, so that the former possesses, to an appalling degree, the power to deal oppressively with the latter.

" 4. In the view to which political economy is restricted, no intervention can be recognized ; and, consequently, although this oppressive power that attaches to the possession of capital is seldom exercised to its possible extreme, yet our prevailing social doctrines, being narrowed to the limitations of political economy, give a theoretical sanction to the extremest exercise of that power.

" 5. But there is nevertheless an intervention that must be acknowledged, proceeding out of the moral intelligence of society, which develops rules of just conduct in the place of rules of conduct that are purely selfish.

" 6. This moral intelligence has now attained culture enough to produce a common notion of justice, in the face of which *might* can no longer be claimed to make right, no matter in what attributes the endowment of *might* may be conferred.

" 7. Hence, even though the possessors of wealth had acquired it as a consequence of capabilities in which they are superior to their fellows who acquire no wealth, still the vast advantage which that acquisition throws into their

hands cannot be recognized as belonging to them
with absoluteness and by right, to be exercised at
will, and under the dictation of their self-interest
alone.

"8. But a large part of the wealth and capital of the world is gathered into the hands of
its possessors either by no active exertion of any
kind on their own part, or by methods of acquisition which are sometimes pure robbery and sometimes removed only a step or two from it ; and,
for all this large part, even that claim of right to
the advantage which capital holds over dependent
labor cannot reasonably be set up.

"9. On the whole, therefore, we may safely
conclude it to be not in accordance with true principles of justice and right, that the terms of copartnership in production, between the capitalist
and the laborer, should be left wholly for settlement to a compromise between the self-interest of
the former and the inexorable necessities of the
latter.

"Do you accept this," said the judge, when he
had finished reading, " as a fair summing up of
our talk, and are we agreed thus far in our conclusions ? "

" I accept and assent," said I, and so said all
the company.

" Well, then," continued the judge, " we will
proceed. We have determined, somewhat to our

satisfaction, that the capitalist may not rightfully
exact from the laborer all that he has power to
exact, when the joint product of capital and labor
is divided between them; and now, of course, we
shall have to determine, as nearly as we can, how
much he may demand, with justice, for himself.

"But, first, I wish to consider with you a little
further, and just for a moment, the question of
rights between that wealth which is actually acquired by superior capability, and that poverty
which is the consequence of a want of capability.
It is very hard for the human mind, self-environed
as it is, to give up the primitive idea that a man is
entitled to all the benefits of every advantage that
he can get from better faculties than his neighbors
have. We cannot, therefore, reach too much distinctness on this point.

"Now, the faculties which contribute to success in the acquisition of wealth, by justifiable
methods, are widely diversified faculties; but, generally speaking, how would you rank them among
the faculties of the human being? Looking around
among the men of your acquaintance who are
called 'successful men,' and who have acquired
fortune or pecuniary independence by strictly un-
exceptionable means, as we estimate in these matters, what should you say of the faculties to which
their acquisition of wealth has been due? Are
they of a highly superior kind, as compared with

4

other human faculties which do not enter into money-making?"

"No," replied I, "I have often thought of that. The men who bring to bear in 'business,' of production or exchange, any really superior intellectual force, seem to be few — I mean comparatively few. There is hardly any other object of human exertion that does not call out higher capabilities. I think it is rather seldom—though it sometimes happens — that a man who has capabilities of the higher order can concentrate them on this object of money-getting. Their focus is not easily adjusted to it. But it is the concentration of a man's forces that tells, in everything; and that man, therefore, whose energies are of such a disposition that they will bend themselves freely and fully to this object, is the successful man in acquiring wealth, even though the faculties thus compacted may be inferior to the faculties of his unsuccessful neighbor. As a rule, I should say—with many exceptions, however—the money-making faculties and qualities are quite of a narrow kind, with very frequent littleness and ignobility; but the energy in them and the activity behind them are usually intense. The character of man compounded in this way is an exceedingly useful one, but not in the highest degree an admirable one."

"Very true," returned the judge, "and hence

we see that the capable powers among men which
win, in the one great struggle that pits them all
against each other—the struggle, that is, to eman-
cipate themselves from daily servitude to their
bodily wants—are not necessarily, nor as a rule,
the higher faculties of man, nor those that would
seem most deserving. On the other hand, a want
of capability in the acquisition of wealth is plainly
no proof of an inferior man, nor of a man whose
contributions to society are of little worth. The
inventors, the scientific discoverers, the originators
of new methods and new ideas, the path-finders of
commerce, the philosophers, the poets, the men of
learning, of literature and of art—all the pioneers
and guides of human progress, in a word, are well-
nigh invariably men who cannot or do not get a
fair share of the wealth of the world in return for
their services to it. It is almost a law, in fact, that
no man can possess and exercise any faculty of
general value to mankind without being rendered
nearly impotent so far as the gathering of wealth
to himself is concerned. I will venture further,
and say that it *is* a law, with not many exceptions ;
it holds good, you will find, from top to bottom
in the whole range of diversified human capabilities. A man cannot be a good artisan or mechanic,
in any kind of hand-labor which makes the least
demand upon intelligent faculties, without concen-
trating so much of all his powers upon the imme-

diate object of his labor, that he is compelled to trust its ultimate results, so far as his own benefit is concerned, to other agencies. If he is to be a good workman, he can withhold from his work neither time enough, nor thought enough, nor will enough, to make combinations of trade, or to conduct speculations, or to organize the conjoining of his own labor with the labor of others. All this he must trust those whose business it is, to do for him. For his own part, he can only do good work, of the kind he has chosen to do, and deliver it in commission, as I may say, to such industrial and commercial system as prevails, taking whatever return that system may render to him. If this man tries to 'make money' in any other way than by industriously doing good work, of such kind as he is best fitted to do, it must be at the expense of his proper work, and a certain loss to the world of true, efficient, productive workmanship ensues.

"Do you not see, therefore, that an industrial system which puts a great premium on the exercise of those special but not eminent faculties that are employed in what we describe by the general term 'business,' is an economically vicious system, as well as an unjust one? In our use of the word 'business,' we mean by it—1. The organizing, or the effectively putting together, of the labor of different persons, as in manufactories or in transportation; 2. Trade, or the conducting of exchanges between different producers, and between producers and non-producing consumers; 3. Financial business, monetary dealings, the manipulating of that movable, current capital which is the life-blood of industry and commerce. Now, the faculties that are employed in these ways do so monopolize, under present conditions, the acquisition and the accumulation of wealth, that it is well-nigh impossible for men to extort more than a decent living by the employment of other faculties, in all the other greater fields of human industry, intelligence, and energy. Do you not see what a profoundly distracting and depressing influence this exerts upon those purely productive faculties which these 'business' faculties, as we will call them, ought to be in cordial and helpful coöperation with? Do you not see that the men who could best be mechanics, inventors, designers, and so on, are under a perpetual temptation to try to be merchants, tradesmen, managers of business, speculators, and the like; while men who do become artisans and mechanics, in a fit calling, are perpetually drawn away from a fervent concentration of themselves upon their work by dreams of easier fortune, and the contriving of plans for making more gain in other ways?"

"I do, indeed," said I; "we can, none of us, help seeing the effect, for it is becoming more conspicuous every day; and it is cried out against every day without being rightly understood. The young men of successive generations seem to become more reluctant to commit themselves to mechanical callings in life, or to directly productive labor of any kind, and prefer to scramble, in crowds which grow greater every year, for clerkships, for footholds and places of the poorest sort in the ' business '-world. It is the universal complaint, too, that mechanic workmanship of every kind is deteriorating in its quality. It certainly is difficult, nowadays, to get good and thorough work done in any department of manual industry."

"To be sure," said the judge, "and I am convinced that the desertion and deterioration of mechanical industries will continue to be an increasing evil until we have begun, in some way, to cut down the excessive premium which our present adjustment of relationships between capital and labor puts upon those faculties and energies that enter into what we distinguish from other labor by calling it ' business.' The crowds will swarm, of course, where the prizes are distributed. So long as the substantial rewards of exertion are seen to be displayed, almost entirely, in the market-booths and in the counting-houses, in the office and at the desk, instead of in the shop and at the work-bench, you may be sure that the office and the counting-house, the store and the bank, will be mobbed with young applicants; and you

may be sure, too, that there will be a lowering of
ambition and a lessening of spirit in the work
which is done at the bench, at the anvil, and in
the factory. It cannot be otherwise. All the influences that act upon labor, under present conditions, seem to me to be profoundly depressing on
the mechanics and the operatives.

"There is evidently bad economy, as well as
injustice, in the industrial system which has this
outcome. Society cannot afford to continue giving
such excessive encouragement to one set of human
faculties as against all the others which unitedly contribute to its material progress. Sooner or
later it must contrive in some way to make those
several faculties which produce, on one side, the
skillful, ingenious mechanic, the adept artisan, the
capable clerk, the efficient laborer of any plodding
sort, and which produce, on the other side, the
organizer, the merchant, the financier, the 'man
of business'—it must contrive in some way, I say,
to make these several faculties serve one another
on fairer terms; to make them serve one another
on terms more nearly proportioned to the value of
what they severally contribute to the product of
the whole."

"Yes," said I; "but how?"

"Ay, there's the rub," replied the judge.
"On principle it is easy to tell how, in general
terms. In practice it is not so easy. I trust the

growing sense of justice among men to slowly work the problem out. There is only one course which the movement toward justice in this matter can take, and that is in the direction of establishing a relation of partnership between the organizers of labor on one hand and the laborers on the other, to supplant the rude relationship in which they now stand toward each other as 'employers' and 'employés.' Employers and employés ! These very terms are significant of the arbitrariness of the system which they represent. In the fair sense of that word, the mechanic in a shop, or the so-called operative in a factory, may just as truly be said to 'employ' the capitalist-proprietor of the factory or the shop to organize the effective combination of his special work with the work of his fellows, and to make the exchange of products for him, as the proprietor may be said to employ *him* to do the special work which he does. The difference between them in the matter of employing each other's services is just that which grows out of a state of dependence on one side and of independence on the other side, whereby all the reciprocity of interest under which these two men, with their differing faculties, ought to be brought to act together, and to serve and assist one another in the great undertakings of human labor, is extinguished. One becomes actually the 'employer,' and one the 'employed,' instead of each being the employer of the capabilities of the other on fairly-adjusted terms. One receives his daily rate of wages, fixed for the most part by the average state of need in his class; the other makes what he can out of the bargain, and drives it hard to make the utmost. It is very plain to me that no equity in the partitioning of the products of human industry can be had under the wages system that we now maintain; under the system, that is, which gives a fixed compensation to one side, while profits, indefinite, unshared and unaccounted for, go wholly to the other."

"What, then," I asked, "can take the place of the 'wages system?' Do you look to the 'cooperative system' for your remedy?"

"No, I do not," returned the judge; "if you mean that plan of association among working-men in which they undertake to conduct for themselves the business incident to their own work. I do not expect much from that 'coöperative system,' notwithstanding the remarkable successes it has shown at Rochdale and in other instances, both in England and on the Continent. It is an attempt on the part of men who represent the mechanical, constructive, producing faculties, to dispense with the coöperation of men who represent the organizing, combining, commercial faculties, and I hold that these two sets of faculties are indispensable to one another. The mechanic working-man almost always, under present conditions, *is* a work-ing-man, in the received sense of the word, simply because he has no aptitude nor training for the shrewd arithmetic of commerce, and competes at a disadvantage, for that reason, in the scrambling division of worldly goods. Now it is clearly impossible for a number of men in this luckless strait to gain much by going into league with one another, to make a common cause of the common disadvantage under which they are struggling. You surely cannot evolve such a thing as a corporate capability for traffic or industrial management by any conceivable multiplication together of individual incapabilities. You may put sixpences and shillings enough together to form the capital that will create and sustain an iron foundery or a cotton-mill; but in a body of men whose efficient faculty of accumulation is limited to the mere saving of sixpences and shillings, where are you going to find, or how are you going to develop, the faculty that can handle such a capital and work profitable results out of it? This 'co-operative' theory of industrial reform is totally fallacious, in my judgment, because it makes no account of the competition of faculties out of which the whole problem arises. As I look at the matter, the only coöperation that can possibly achieve any equitable social change is coöperation between the faculties of the artisan and the faculties of the man of business, established upon any terms that shall make a common cause between them, in place of the competition and antagonism to which they are necessarily committed under our present industrial system. That is what I mean when I speak of the organization of capital and labor upon a footing of copartnership.

"Mind you, I do not claim an equal copartnership; for equity and equality, as I have said before, are two very different things. I am not a communist, nor an agrarian, nor a social revolutionist of any sort. I do not want to abolish property, nor riches, nor poverty even, so far as poverty is a just consequence of the inefficient or unfaithful performance of a man's part in the work of the world. Equality of goods I have no wish to see brought about; I would not have it in society if I could. All that I contend for, as being necessary to justice between the workingman and the business-man—between the laborer and the capitalist—is that fundamental equality of footing, in their relations to one another, which the terms of any sort of copartnership between them will establish, no matter how insignificant at first may be the benefit to the former. Anything, to begin with, that will engraft a different principle upon this wages system of ours, under which men are mere marketable machines for such and such work, selling themselves by the day or the year, instead of being sold for a lifetime as the slaves were."

"I suppose, then," said I, "that you hope for the success and spread of the experiment which has already been somewhat tried, in a few proprietary industrial establishments, of making dividends from the annual profits of the concern to the working-men employed?"

"Yes, that is my hope. These experiments furnish proof," continued the judge, "that some consciousness of the inequity, and some perception of the vicious economy of the prevailing wages system, have begun to be awakened, and I am confident that both the moral feeling and the enlightened judgment which are to condemn that system will gain a steady growth. I am not at all surprised that these experiments in the organizing of a partnership between the working-men and the managing capitalist, who supplies and directs their work, have sometimes failed. We are sure to hear more of the failures than of the successes, and, although some of them may belong in the ordinary category of business failures, consequent upon adverse times or unsound management, they are naturally enough all charged against the experiment to which they are incident. In many cases, without doubt, the failure is rightly so charged. There is much to be practically learned before a successful adjustment of dividends from

their joint production can be made between labor
and capital, and between the laborer and the manager.

"The working-men have much to learn. I am
not blind at all to the obstacles which their preva-
lent ignorance of the conditions of production
and trade, and their characteristic inaptitude for
knowledge or appreciation of what we call business affairs, throw in the way of a reformation of
the industrial system. There are comparatively
few among them who apprehend in the slightest
degree the just merits of their own cause. Their
demands and their whole attitude, taking them as
a class, are generally unreasoning and provocative
of the very antagonism by which they are wronged.
I quite believe that the selfishness of capital can
more easily be overcome than this blind unreason
on the labor-side. It will resist with less obsti-
nacy, perhaps, the generous, harmonizing forces
that are at work in human culture. But I know
that those forces are invincible, and that they will
have their way in the end. It is but a question
of time. The ferment of the age compels all
men to learn. The capitalist, on his part, will
learn the wisdom of magnanimity in using his
power—the expediency of justice; and the working-man, on his part, will learn to understand the
conditions by which production is governed, and
to estimate his dues from it by some logical reck-

oning. But he may have to learn through bitter teachings of experience, as I fear that he must, because his class is being blindly led now into a conflict with the very laws of industrial economy, under which its own rights must be adjudicated and established."

"I begin to see, sir," remarked John, "that your views are not so radically extreme as they seemed to be at first. The 'labor question,' as you look at it, holds itself quite above the issues that are nowadays being raised in the industrial world between labor and capital, and you do not sympathize, I take it, with the 'trades-union' combinations, which interfere so mischievously with almost every important branch of productive enterprise."

"Yes, I do sympathize with them," said the judge, "in a sorrowful way. I sympathize deeply with the discontented feeling, on the part of the working-class, out of which they spring, and it is very sad to me to see these people, who have become conscious that there is something wrong in their relations to the industry to which they contribute, misconceiving so entirely the nature of the wrong and aggravating it by mistaken means of remedy. They organize a revolt against—they know not what. Not against the wages system, for they affirm that, and confirm it, and rivet upon themselves by every measure which they adopt.

They exert their combined influence to suppress the individualization of skill and faculty, which would tend, in a powerful way, to break down the systematic fixity of this wages-paying custom. They level down to one mean average all the different degrees of the efficient value of labor which they severally represent in their several. trades; and such an average is sure to be depressed toward the minimum extreme, by the least skillful, the least conscientious, the least intelligent labor in every trade. It is pitiful to see the mistake which so many of the working-men make in their trades-unions, when they combine to enforce and maintain any uniform rate of wages, and so suppress, as far as possible, among themselves, all competitive ambition—all competition of faculty and spirit in their own ranks. By this course they leave little inducement for any working-man to excel in his work, either through the acquirement of knowledge and skill, or through industrial conscientiousness. So far as they can, they put the most skilled and most efficient workman upon the same footing with the laziest, the most careless and the least capable. It is a woful mistake in its effect upon the character of the working-class, and therefore in its effect upon the standing and strength and social condition of the class."

"But is that the worst mistake of the trades-unions?" asked I.

"Yes," replied the judge, " because it is their fundamental mistake. Almost everything else which they wrongly do originates in this and forms part of it. There is more than a mistake in some of their measures; there is the nature of crime. There is a criminal violation of their own industrial rights: as when they undertake, for example, by their rules and by the influential power of their combination, to restrict the liberty which belongs to each man to control the disposition of his own labor; when they assume to dictate to their members the terms upon which each one shall work, and to say when and where and how he shall accept employment, and when and where and how he shall not: also, when they assume to legislate for any branch of industry concerning its hours of labor, the number of apprentices or pupils that shall be annually received into its several establishments, and other matters of that sort, touching which there can be no conceivable right of interference with individual liberty lodged anywhere, neither in any particular body of men nor in the whole body of society. I would not have much intervention of law in dealing with matters pertaining to the organization and regulation of the industrial system of a country, but I would have all such interferences with individual freedom as these, whether by combinations on the side of labor or on the side of capital, rigorously suppressed, by stringent prohibitions of law, stringently enforced."

"And what of labor 'strikes,' " said I; "how do you regard them ? "

"I can only condemn them," replied the judge, "so far as they are coercively organized. It is assuredly every man's right to refuse to labor for another, or in coöperation with another, if the terms proposed are not satisfactory to him; provided he can afford to refuse, and does not make himself dependent upon the charity of his fellows for support by refusing. It is equally the right of a number of men to voluntarily combine in refusing to work on given terms, if they are unitedly able to support themselves for a certain time without work; and it is their right under many circumstances to make the pressure of their abstention from work bear as hard as, by voluntary union, it can be made to bear upon the interests of employing capital, for the purpose of extorting better terms. But there are not many labor-strikes, I think, in which coercion of some sort is not employed to bring about the union of those who take part in it. A few restless, dominating spirits get leadership in the matter, by sheer dogmatic and dictatorial force, and a most tyrannical constraint is often exercised upon the minority, if not upon the majority, of the members of the industrial organization concerned. The workman who prefers to continue in employment on the existing terms, rather than become idle, or who feels that he cannot afford to surrender employment, and that the suffering to be imposed upon his family by such surrender involves a deeper wrong than the one against which he is asked to array himself in revolt, finds usually among his associates in his own class no toleration whatever of his personal rights, interests, or convictions of duty. His claim to individual freedom of action is resented and resisted with all the tremendous forces of hostility and oppression which any class organization can bring to bear upon its members. If he does not suffer personal violence from his fellows, as he very often does, he suffers a persecuting ostracism which is even harder to bear up against. It is by such coercion, I think, that most 'strikes' are brought about, and they are generally more tyrannical and more cruel, I am afraid, than the wrongs in wages-paying which they undertake to redress. The men who set them on foot seem to be commonly of the mischief-making sort—disturbers, agitators, demagogues. They are men of an energetic and combative disposition, without much judgment, and without much scruple, sometimes. They love strife and turbulence; they find their congenial element in such a state of things, and they gain some importance when they bring it about. Such men are no doubt actuated more by vanity and by their appetite for controversy than they are by any intelligent sense of rights and wrongs, or by any conscientious solicitude for the interests of the working-class. They do not represent the judgment or the feeling of that class, and yet the imperious, combative energy which they possess wins for them a kind of leadership in it that is undoubtedly mischievous. The same kind of fact exhibits itself in every department of society—conspicuously in its political formations, where the positive, dogmatic, aggressive, and not very scrupulous politicians are apt to override better counsels in public affairs and have their way. It is not strange, therefore, that labor-strikes are commonly miscalculated and mistimed; that they are so often aggressive rather than defensive; that there is so often more of malice than of self-assertion in their spirit; that they are so often aimed at mischief to the capitalist rather than benefit to the laborer; that they so often represent a fatuous revolt against the fundamental laws of production and exchange, and that their effect so often is locally destructive or injurious to the industries in which they occur. Theoretically, the labor-strike is a legitimate measure of self-defense and self-assertion on the part of the laboring-class against the managing-capitalist class, under their present relations to one another; but, practically, I am afraid, it is a measure seldom wisely or honestly resorted to."

"I think that is true," remarked John, "and the working-men seem to exhibit just as much of a disposition to use their opportunities against capital in a grinding, oppressive, and aggressive way, as the capitalists do, on their side, to make a hard use of the advantages which they hold over labor. They do it with less judgment, too, and with a kind of vindictiveness which does not appear on the other side. They so often organize their strikes in some department of production just when the investors of capital in that department are struggling hard against adverse conditions in it, and make demands which all the circumstances of the market then surrounding the particular industry in question render it wholly impossible to accede to. At other times they fatuously serve the selfish interests of their employers, by interrupting some industry which the capitalists engaged in it are very glad to have suspended, so that there seems to be good reason, in frequent cases, for suspecting that the employers have secretly instigated the strike, and thus have brought about a check upon production without responsibility or cost to themselves. It is hardly to be wondered at that this blindness and folly and mischievous disposition in the laboring-classes loses sympathy for them among intelligent lookers-on, and produces an antagonistic feeling in the ranks of the employing capitalists."

"No," said the judge, "it is all natural
enough, and that is the troublesome feature of
the problem in its present stage. The meaner
parts of human nature are involved on both sides
of it. There is just as much selfishness and just
as much narrow one-sidedness of consideration on
the part of the laborers as there is on the part of
the capitalists, with more ignorance, but with less
power. I give attention chiefly to those wrongs
in the relationship between the two which the
capitalists and managers of our industrial organization are responsible for, because they represent
the stronger side. They hold the power, so much
more than the others do, to act wrongfully, and
their duty is commensurate with their power.
Between two parties, in any system of wrongs,
the movement of redress and remedy must come
from the stronger one. The most potent moral
influence in the world is that of magnanimity proceeding out of power, and we must invoke that
in this matter before any solution of the problem
can be possible. Let the managers and holders of
capital begin to acknowledge that the measure of
their power is not the measure of their just rights,
by beginning to associate the working-men in interest with them, under some system of partnership, with some system of dividends introduced to
supplement the wages system—and the moment
they do this, I know that the working-men will be-

gin to be inquisitive for themselves about the circumstances and conditions on which their several industries depend. They will begin to observe and apprehend the phenomena of the market, out of which the laws of industrial economy are deduced. They will begin to understand better the terms on which their particular labor is associated with all other labor in the industrial organization of the civilized world. They will do so on account of having become partners instead of servitors in the several industries, by virtue of which change they will have necessarily acquired an independent personal interest in such matters of knowledge. They must then be inspired by every personal motive to act in coöperation with the managers of capital, in their several branches of productive industry, and the desire to coöperate will be effective in promoting their intelligence.

"This industrial reform is one in which there must be preaching as well as teaching, and the preaching comes first in importance; wherefore I prefer now to act the preacher. Political economy alone is not enough, as I have said before. Social ethics has quite as much to do with the question, if not more. We must preach the doctrine of justice, as well as teach the laws of production and trade.

"It will not do much good to go to the trades-union with instructions in political economy, so

long as its members are made distrustful of all
your formulas by a vague and rankling consciousness of something arbitrary in the system of the
division of industrial products, which political
economy gives countenance to. We must first
root out of public sentiment the old barbaric notion that—

> ' He may take who has the power,
> And he may keep who can.'

We must root it out just as completely with reference to the power which attaches to wealth, to
possessory rights, to superior mercantile faculties, and to superior opportunities in acquisition,
as we have already rooted it out, among civilized
men, with reference to the brute power which be-
longed of old to bodily strength and baronial cas-
tles, to the lance, the sword, and the coat of mail.
We must educate public opinion to recognize just
rights in the matter which law cannot enforce, but
which its own silent legislation may affirm and
make good.

" Then political economy may hope to win the
ear of the working-man and reach his understanding. Then the trades-union may be made to become a powerful organism in the industrial world,
and be brought out of conflict into coöperation
with capital, in the productive enterprises of society. The guilds of the mediæval craftsmen were

institutions of splendid usefulness in many respects. The modern trades-unions may be the same, and more, in much the same direction. I look forward to the time when they will be encouraged to take upon themselves the responsible guardianship of all the interests of the mechanic industries—each its own; fixing and maintaining a high standard of excellence in workmanship for every trade; graduating the mechanics in their several arts and conferring diplomas and degrees, as the colleges do, with such strictness and fairness and authority that the classifications of the union or guild shall be recognized in the labor-market; opening their doors to all new-comers widely, without any bars except such as these standards of proficiency will set up; aiming to individualize—not generalize—the compensation of labor in each department of work, by individualizing the labor itself; looking always to the efficiency, the skill, the productive value, of each man's work for the basis of the apportionment of dividends to him from the production to which he contributes.

"You may say that I am visionary; but remember that I am only trying to define the state of things which must be brought about, as it seems to me, if the just harmony of rights and interests between labor and capital is ever to be attained. I do not expect it very soon. I am not sure that we are within ten centuries of it yet. I am not sure, in fact, that it will ever be reached. But I do have a strong faith, nevertheless, in the final completeness of the evolution of justice among men, before human history ends, and I am willing to be called visionary in that, if you please to consider me so."

The judge rose as he finished speaking, and, in his prompt way, took leave of us for the evening, so that we had no opportunity to reply to his last remarks.

5

FOURTH EVENING.

The Increase of Production within a Century past.—The Judge's Estimates.—Machine-Labor and its Results.—The Working-man's Measure of Gain.—Wasteful Consumption.—What it is and what Kind of Waste can be socially restrained.—The Sources of Increase to the Capital Fund, and of Increased Dividends to Labor.

WHEN the judge came he was a little late, and excused himself by saying that he had taken time to look up a few passages in the political economists, touching points which he thought we should now have to consider, and especially with reference to the so-called " wages-fund," by which the compensation of labor is said to be limited. I laughed at this, and rubbed my hands with some show of glee. " Now you are coming to hard work, judge," said I. " I have been thinking of the rough road that we should put you upon when we began to ask questions, as to the source from which you expect to derive a substantial and permanent increase of dividends to the laboring-men of all classes. If there is any sure fact in political economy, I should say it is that which is stated in the description of what is called the ' wages-fund : ' the fact, namely, that at any given time there is a certain tolerably definite appropriation made out of the accumulations from past labor to maintain present production ; that there cannot be divided among the producing laborers of that time, either in wages or otherwise, anything exceeding this appropriation, and that their several shares from it must be, on the average, according to the proportion between their total numbers and the total sum. How can it be otherwise ? I do not see that you can put any moral restraint, any more than you can put a legal restraint, upon unproductive consumption. If you are able to make it a matter of recognized duty that no man shall profligately and wastefully consume the products of labor in idle luxury, you cannot define the duty. You cannot mark points where it begins and where it ends. You cannot even define for any one producing member of society a limit of productive consumption, beyond which his consumption shall be set down as unproductive. The food, the clothing, and the shelter of the producer belong, of course, within the range of his productive consumption ; but what kind of food ?—what kind of clothing ?—what kind of shelter ? What latitude of selection and variation shall he have within recognized bounds

of productive consumption? And then his education and his culture are just as much objects of productive consumption as the feeding and protecting
of his body are, because they contribute to his productive efficiency and capacity. How much shall be
allowed for these? How much schooling? How
many books? How much travel? How much
leisure for observation and comparison? How
much recreation to preserve the elasticity of his
energies? How much exercise of hospitality?
How many household conveniences, and refine-
ments, and adornments? How many artistic indul-
gences? How much gratification of rational
tastes? Where shall we say that productive consumption ends, in his case, and unproductive consumption begins? We cannot say. It must be
impossible, therefore, to define any rule of duty
for governing the consumption of the products of
labor. The broad rule which condemns profligacy
and wastefulness cannot be reduced to a definite
standard. Those who command possession of the
products of labor are left substantially free to consume them as they please. The share which they
will reserve from their personal consumption, year
by year, and dedicate to renewed production, must
depend upon the inducements to accumulation by
which they are acted on ; and those inducements
are very nearly constant in their influence upon
men in a given state of civilization. I do not see

how we can materially strengthen them, or materially augment their effect; and I do not see, therefore, how we can bring about any considerable increment of the ' wages-fund,' or the capital out of which labor is to be paid, proportionately to the number of those who have to draw their compensation from it. If you can tell me, my dear judge, pray do so at once, for I am impatient to learn."

" I must admit," replied the judge, " that this is no easy part of our subject which we are approaching now. We are coming into fogs that are sometimes pretty thick. I have groped in them, and stumbled and traveled round and round in bewilderment without making headway, a great many times. But I think that if we use our eyes steadily we can gather some light out of the murky confusion to guide us, nevertheless.

" The first thing to be certain about, no doubt, is whether labor has or has not become productive enough to furnish the means for any considerable increase of dividends to labor, without resorting to communism, or the equal partitioning of goods, which I do not believe in at all; without interfering, in fact, with the inequalities of wealth that are just, nor diminishing in the slightest degree the inducements which stimulate even the greatest accumulation of wealth by honest means. What do you think about that ? "

"Well," said I, "it is certain that the productiveness of labor has been enormously augmented since the present century began, by the mechanical devices which we call labor-saving, although it would be more proper to describe them as labor-helping. But the capacity for consumption in the human race seems to outrun its capacity for production, no matter how the latter may be quickened. New wants are developed by the ability to supply them, even faster than the supplying capability evolves itself, so that those who can command the enjoyment of their desires may absorb the products of labor as freely as they ever did. We evidently cannot surfeit human desires, and we seem, therefore, to be making no progress toward the production of a surplus beyond the greed of the greedy, out of which it will be any easier to make a generous dividend to the dependent laborers of the world than it was a thousand years ago. The conditions of the struggle for existence, relatively considered, seem to remain about the same, after all the gain in productiveness that has accrued to civilized labor."

"That may be true," returned the judge, "but we will consider the point hereafter. What I wish to look at now is simply the fact of the enormously-increased and increasing productiveness of labor, which is surely a fact of tremendous import in human history. I do not think that we, any of

us, realize the magnitude of the increase and the
cumulative ratio at which it has been going on
since the Aryan intellect began to be scientifically
exercised, and its inventive faculties were brought
fairly into play. If we could exactly know how
many workmen would have been necessary two
hundred years ago, with the processes and ap-
pliances of that age, to furnish in a given time the
products that are now turned out in the same time
by the labor of England, France, Germany, and
the United States, we should doubtless be as-
tounded by the figures. It would be hard, however, to gather the data for even an approximate
calculation of the sort; because every present product represents such complicated intermixings of
labor. In the case of a product of machine-work,
for example, there enters into it all the successive,
multifarious operations of industry by which the
metals and wood composing the material of the
machine in question were produced and brought
together; then the inventing and experimenting
by which this machine was perfected; then, behind these, another complication of the same factors of labor in the other machines which have contributed help in the making of this particular one;
and so on, indefinitely, almost. If we were able
to thus determine the quantity of human labor
which the machine itself represents, from first to
last, going back, very likely, to years before it was

ever dreamed of, we should then have to distribute this by equal division over the whole product of its work, from the time it was first set in motion until it wears itself out, with allowance made for repairs and improvements meantime. That done, we should next have to trace out the innumerable tributary industries which have entered into the production and bringing together of the materials upon which the machine operates, or which it is employed to fashion into a given shape; and these, in most cases, will include, first and last, the work of farmers, miners, machinists, inventors, scientific discoverers, merchants, bankers, clerks, shipbuilders, sailors, railroad engineers, and mechanics and working men in a hundred avocations at least.

"The calculation is manifestly an impossible one, and any attempt to determine how much the productive efficiency of human labor has been multiplied within a given time can only be guesswork at the best. We can keep our estimates safely within reason, however, and have enough, perhaps, to found all necessary conclusions upon.

"An effort was made not long ago by Dr. Engel, the director of the Prussian Statistical Bureau, to procure statistics of the steam-power in use in the world. He was only partially successful, but from the data gathered he estimated—if the report that I have seen is correct—that there cannot be less than from three to three and a half

millions of horse-power at work in the stationary
engines of the world, and ten millions of horse-
power in the land locomotive engines. The marine
engines add considerable to this, but I shall not
take them into account at present. Now, this
steam power which is at work on the continental
portions of the globe—most of it in Europe and
America—drawing loads, lifting burdens, forging
metals, grinding corn, whirling spindles and driving the shuttles in a million of looms, is so much
force, brought to the help of human labor, which
is maintained without any consumption of animal
or vegetable food. The feeding of it is from
mineral stores laid up in the bowels of the earth ;
its activity draws nothing from the resources of
the soil of the globe, except to the extent of the
food of the miners who dig the coal which is
burned in the engine-furnace, and the force maintained in their muscles is to the force generated by
the product of their labor as one to a thousand, at
most. This is an important fact to consider in
connection with what we are discussing, because
the limits to vegetation on the soil-surface of the
earth are the chief limits imposed upon human
labor. This steam labor-force, which is fed with
coals instead of with grains or grasses, is equal to
the working force of about 25,000,000 horses, because the theoretical ' horse-power' of the steam
engine is nearly equivalent to the average actual

working power of two horses, according to the calculations now most accepted. Hence, to do the same work, of transportation, of lifting, of grinding, of crushing, and of moving machinery which acts in the place of human fingers and hands, 25,000,000 horses would have to be employed—supposing that horses were capable of the same work, with the same steadiness and celerity and in the same efficient way, which they are not. The horse consumes, I should say, as much food, at least, as three men. It is true that man's food ordinarily costs more labor than that of the horse, because he wants a greater variety in it, and employs labor to bring him tea from China, coffee from Java, sugar from the West Indies, etc.; but, relatively to the producing capabilities of the soil of the earth, a horse must consume not less than three times as much as a man, and competes with man in that ratio for the subsistence which the earth yields. To put steam-power therefore in the place of 25,000,000 horses is equivalent to a saving of food for about 75,000,000 human beings more than could otherwise be fed from the same area of soil, under the same state of cultivation. This is not, my dear sir, a mere matter of idle speculation ; for statisticians have found that, in all civilized countries of the world, the rate of increase in the number of horses has diminished greatly since the introduction of steam-power began to be rapid and

universal, which was less than half a century ago.
The effect was first noticed in Europe, I believe,
but it has become strongly marked in this country,
as well.   From 1850 to 1860 the increase of horses
in the United States was at the rate of 44 per
cent., but from 1860 to 1870 it fell to 14 per cent.
Something must be allowed, no doubt, for the
effects of the war in the last decade, but not
enough to account for half this great decrease.   It
represents the progress of the substitution of in-
animate for animate dumb servants in the employ
of man.   I do not care to predict that this will go
so far as to displace all domestic animals from
working service, but I can see that invention is
pushing the horse and the ox out of employment
very fast, and that every year the sweep of this
effect appears to extend.   We are now just at the
point, it would seem, of having the steam-engine
fully adapted to canal navigation, to street-car
locomotion, to ploughing and general farm work
and even to draft service on common roads.   In
my view, this movement of substitution is one of
vast importance and significance, not only because
it augments the efficiency of labor, but because it
tends toward the taking of brute animals out of
competition with man as consumers of the products
of the soil, and thus enormously increases the stock
which remains for division among the human producers.   Do you agree with me so far as this?"

" I do," said I. " The fact which you have
brought to notice has all the significance that you
claim for it, I think, and it becomes very interesting to me, as well as very important, in that view,
which I have never seen presented before."

" Very well, then," continued the judge, " we
will go on: the stationary steam-engines in the
world, which have come into existence almost
wholly within the last half century, and more than
half of them, probably, within the last twenty
years, are doing a great variety of work; but
chiefly they are employed in propelling machinery
which performs mechanical operations that formerly had to be performed by the fingers, hands
and arms of working-men and working-women.
Along with these steam-engines, there is also being
employed, in the same kind of work, an enormous
water-power, the machinery for utilizing which
has been improved within our own generation almost as greatly as the machinery for utilizing the
expansive power of steam has been ; and this represents, even more than steam does, a non-consum-
ing force, doing prodigious work for man without
drawing much from the productive resources of
the soil. The water-power in use is fully equal,
perhaps, to the steam-power, and both of these
mighty servants are driving machines which man
has only to wait upon and watch and direct, and
which execute, under his supervision and with his

help, each within its own specialized function, all the way from five to a thousand times the quantity of a given work which he could do with his unaided hands.

"In such simple mechanical operations as the cutting of nails, the making of needles and pins, and the stamping of metals into shapes—where power and precision in one quick monotonous movement are the only requisites—the multiplication of product by machine labor over hand labor is very great. In constructive processes where a combination of movements is necessary, the multiplication of product is less, and proportionately so, I suspect, to the mechanical complications involved. But the division of machine labor is being organized to perfection, in the same way as the division of human labor, and the constant tendency, in almost every branch of manufacture, is toward the resolving of one complicated machine into two or three or four simple ones, each of which performs a single operation by a single movement, thus gaining the maximum effect of power, precision and uniform speed.

"But even in the more complex constructive operations, the gain of product from a given quantity of human labor, employed as auxiliary to machine labor, is immense. Take the making of fabrics for clothing, for example. The power-looms now used at Manchester, England, for the manufacture of common cotton goods, are each said to produce daily, on the average, twenty-six pieces of cotton cloth, twenty-nine yards long and twenty-five inches wide. One person can attend to three of these looms, so that the joint daily product of the man and the machine is seventy-eight pieces; whereas, on the old hand-loom of 1800, one man, working one loom, produced only four pieces. Here, from the same expenditure of human labor, we have a multiplication of product almost twentyfold—less the labor which is represented in the improved machine, in the engine which drives it and in the fuel which the engine consumes, dividing that labor down to the small fraction which is chargeable against one day's work of the machine, out of the thousands of days' work it is capable of doing before it is worn out. We shall make a large allowance for the capitalized labor in this machinery if we set down the final multiplication of product, consequent upon the improvement of mechanical aids to the human laborer, at fifteenfold.

"In the spinning and weaving of woollen cloths and all finer fabrics, the production of a given number of workmen has been multiplied, no doubt, in a ratio somewhat less; but still it must be quite within reason to estimate the average multiplication at tenfold.

"When we pass to consider the making of

these fabrics into clothing, we come upon the most striking mechanical achievement of our own generation—the sewing-machine. I shall ask the ladies here to say how many needle-women one of them is equal to, in efficient work?"

"Not less than ten, I am sure," said my wife.

"I have no doubt that is a moderate statement," continued the judge. "So far, then, as concerns one of the primary wants of man—his clothing—the constructive work, taking all the successive processes after the raw material has been produced, is undoubtedly being now performed by not more than one-tenth of the workmen and workwomen, for a given quantity and kind of product, that were required even fifty or sixty years ago.

"In the matter of shelter—house-building and its allied industries—the fact cannot be very different, although I should make a somewhat lower estimate. Our modern wood-working machinery has wonderfully revolutionized the carpenter's trade. The planing machine, for example, probably performs more work of its kind in a day than twenty industrious journeymen could do with the same precision and perfectness, using hand tools, and, after making a large allowance for the labor capitalized in the machine, in the driving engine, etc., we can safely estimate the multiplica tion of product in this part of building-labor at

fifteenfold. Other kindred machines, like those
for grooving and tonguing, mortising and tenon-
ing, etc., accomplish almost as much, relatively
to hand labor. The mechanical aids in brick-
making have become scarcely less efficient. But
masonry, on the other hand, has not yet acquired
its share of help from the mechanic forces, and so
much hand-work, of fitting together and finishing,
remains in all the branches of building industry,
that the gross average increment of product, com-
paring equal quantities of labor, must be considerably less, for a hundred years past, than in
the department of labor that we considered before.
Taking all the building arts together, including
those which deal with wood, stone and metal, and
including also the furnishings and the fittings of
buildings, I should think it reasonable to estimate
that human labor has now, at least, five times the
productive efficiency that it had a century ago.

" Now let us look at that department of labor
which stands first of all—the department of agricultural labor—the labor which not only produces
the most of man's food, but which produces, also,
the materials on which the greater part of all other
labor expends itself. Here the increment of product, through improved processes and improved
mechanical aids, is necessarily less. The soil is
an independent and stubborn factor of production.
It imposes its own limits upon the labor to

which it responds. It yields more product to more labor, knowingly applied, but it cannot be made to yield proportionately. The ratio of its product to the producing labor grows steadily less as the latter is increased. The one obstinate limit, therefore, which nature has imposed upon the productiveness of human labor is found right here. But even here the achievements of mechanics and science have been prodigious—in three ways: first, by multiplying the effectiveness of a given quantity of labor applied to a given area of soil; secondly, by placing at the command of the tiller of the soil the reënforcement of extra help which he needs, temporarily, at the seasons of planting and harvesting, especially the latter; thirdly, by making wider areas of soil tributary to the wants of given communities, by increasing the facilities of transportation.

"As for the first, even the hand tools of agricultural labor have been improved so much that the very laziest laborer can outstrip with them the hardest-working laborer of a hundred years ago. With the cast-steel plow of to-day, shaped with scientific calculation, to realize the maximum effect from the minimum application of force, the farmer turns far more sod, with the same wear of his horses and of himself, than he could have done with the iron plow of even forty years ago, to say nothing of its clumsier predecessors. Then there are the steam plows, the harrows, the planters, the cultivators, the mowing machines, the reaping machines, the horse rakes, the threshers, the smut-scouring machines, the potato diggers, the ditch diggers, and a score of other contrivances, all of which have come or are coming fast into common use. I have no doubt that, within the regions to which the improved farming of the present day extends, these machines, taken together, have reduced the ordinary working force of men, on given areas of soil, to one-fourth or one-third of the laboring force employed for the same production at the beginning of our century.

"But the second element of productive progress in agriculture which I mentioned a moment ago adds something to the increment.. A given quantity of labor, under the ordinary conditions of agriculture, can prepare soil and plant seeds for a greater crop than the same labor can harvest, during the short season within which the crop has to be gathered and saved, and agriculture was always troubled by this brief periodical need of extra harvesting labor, until the mechanical inventor made a provision for it which involves, simply, the investing of a certain small capital, embodied in certain machines, like the reaper and the mower. It has been estimated that M'Cormick's reaping machine doubled the production of grain in the regions of the West where it was introduced, simply by enabling the available labor of those regions to harvest the crop which it was capable of producing. Without the reaping machine, the farmers would have to lose half of their crop, if they effectively expended all the labor that they could expend in planting and cultivation, or else they would have to withhold one half of the culti- vating labor which they might apply to their farms, in order to produce no greater crop than they were able to gather in. In either case, according to the calculation, the machine saved a waste of pro-ductive labor to the extent of one hundred per cent.; and that reverted effect is quite additional to its own direct effect upon the efficiency of labor while being operated.

"Thirdly and finally, the effectiveness of pro-ductive labor in agriculture has been augmented very greatly by the extraordinary extension and improvement, during late years, of the avenues and vehicles of transportation. The resulting de-crease of time and cost in the carriage of products to distant markets has brought, and is constantly bringing about, more economical divisions of agri-cultural labor, whereby it becomes applied with more and more nearly its maximum effect. When any considerable portion of the lands of some re-gion whose climate and soil are best adapted to wheat-culture has to be devoted to cattle grazing, or to the breeding of sheep, in order to supply local wants, there is a certain waste of the labor thus diverted, because it is being applied with less productive efficiency than it might be. But our railroads, our steam vessels, our canals, and our improved rivers have diminished that waste to an enormous extent during the last half century, and their work is just fairly begun. The wheat-raising, the corn-planting and pork-fattening, the cattle grazing, the sheep breeding, the dairy farming, the fruit culture, and so on, are being districted with the nicest discrimination—with the closest adaptation of the product to climate, soil and every other influential condition—and the area of distributed division is becoming every year more and more continental. You will readily see that this cannot occur without a very great augmentation of the total product, proportionately to the labor expended, even allowing for the auxiliary labor by which such wider exchanges are carried on. The same agency, moreover, is putting a stop to the waste of a localized surplus of product, which used to be common and extensive—as when, for example, the farmers of the West burned for fuel the corn which they could carry to no market.

"Looking over the whole field, at all the improved conditions of agricultural production, I cannot doubt that the efficiency of labor in it has been increased at least fourfold, since no longer ago than last century, in the better civilized countries of the world. That is to say, that, for the same total agricultural product, not less than four times as many laboring hands as are employed in these countries to-day would have had to be employed one hundred years ago. Every successive census shows a relative thinning out of population in the rural districts, wherever these improvements are in progress, and some social philosophers are inspired with great alarm by the increasing tendency of movement in the younger generations of the farm-bred class to 'crowd,' as they say, into cities and towns. They fail to see that it is an inevitable movement, pushed on by the irresistible forces that are at work in society; because it has become impossible to employ on the soil the same proportion of laborers in one generation that was employed the generation before, and each succeeding generation finds the proportion considerably reduced.

"Do you think that my estimate is too large?"

I said that it seemed more likely to be under than above the fact.

"Well, then," proceeded the judge, "let us sum our conclusions up. In the matter of the constructive production of man's clothing, we estimated that the increase of product from given quantities of human labor, as compared with the production of a hundred years ago, has become equal to a multiplication by ten. We estimated a

multiplication by five in the case of labor which produces shelter for him, averaging together all the various kinds of workmanship that are inci-
·dent to the building, fitting and furnishing of his habitations and his houses of business and pleasure. And, finally, we have estimated a multiplication by four in the case of the labor that expends itself in the production of his food, and of such materials derived from the soil as constructive labor is employed upon. Now, I am sure that we are not overstepping the limit of probability if we take the mean multiple of these three to represent the general average increment, within a century, of the productiveness of all labor that is applied to material objects, in those countries, of Europe and America, which are most advanced in the arts and the knowledge of our modern civilization. It seems to me certain that the labor which is productively employed in these countries to-day, putting it all together, is producing at least six times as much as the same number of laborers could have produced a hundred years ago; or, to state the fact differently, that only one man need work now where six worked a hundred years ago to produce the same supply for the satisfaction of human wants to the same extent. If the six do still work, as they certainly do, the multiplication of product, proportionately to the increase of population, is enormous; and if this multiplication is going

on at the same rate, as it appears likely to do, there would seem to be even a possibility of surfeiting, by-and-by, all *rational* wants and desires of the animal man, unless some new rules for the division of the increased product are introduced."

I shook my head.

"Well, no matter," said the judge. "Let that be an open question. I do not care about it. I only care to claim that there is furnished to the race at large, by this vast increase of an always increasing production, enough to improve very considerably the conditions of life for every man who industriously contributes toward it, without interfering at all with the just inequalities of wealth, or impairing at all the effective uses of wealth, or diminishing at all the effective inducements to its accumulation. I am sure that you will agree with me in this?"

I nodded assent and he went on.

"But how much have the conditions of life been improved for the ordinary laborer, or for the average mechanic who works for wages, and who works hard, with no little intelligence and with no small measure of the knowledge of the age in his education? How much does he partake of the stupendous increase of the fruits of labor? I know that he is a partaker;—the poorest beggar, almost, partakes somewhat of the bettered conditions of life; but do you think that, for the wages-paid

mechanic of to-day, there is an augmented share of
comfort and culture and gratification at all equal
to the productive gain of his generation. A few
simple luxuries have been added to his food; but
it is no better, on the whole, nor supplied to him
more abundantly, than it was three hundred years
ago in England, according to Froude, when beef
sold for two farthings a pound, a fat lamb for a
shilling, a chicken for a penny, and wages were
from fourpence to sixpence a day. His house
has gained windows of glass; a chimney to discharge its smoke; a stove or two to equalize its
comfortable warmth; some cheap carpeting in
place of straw upon the floors; softer beds, perhaps, and varnished chairs, instead of benches of
rough-hewn deal. He eats from dishes of a neater
pattern than the wooden trenchers of olden times,
and he has forks and knives to eat with in a decent
way. He has a cheerfuller light in his dwelling
than the rush-light or the tallow dip could give.
His clothing is better fashioned and cleaner that it
used to be. In *body* he is made very comfortable,
no doubt, although he enjoys but sparingly the
conveniences of life which our later times have
been fertile in producing. Books are brought
within his reach, by public libraries and otherwise—if he has time to read them. He may
travel, too, at greatly lessened cost, to see something of the world, and he may gratify all his cu-

rious and inquiring and æsthetic desires at less cost than he formerly could—if he has time. But he is compelled to labor just about as hard and just about as continuously to secure the bodily maintenance and comfort of himself and his family as the laborer did two or three hundred years ago. So the greater part of his share of the improved conditions of life, after all, is just in that improvement of bodily comfort, which does not seem to be very great. Is it enough to fairly account to him for the productive progress of the human race in the last three centuries? I cannot think so. I cannot make myself feel satisfied with it.

" The whole sum total of things which really contribute in any immediate way to the mere maintenance and bodily comfort of the race is produced, we must remember, by a fraction only of the labor of the present day. There has not been a single generation, in the civilized countries, for two hundred years past, at least, which directed over half its labor to that end, and *we* certainly have disengaged more than half of the labor of our time from those objects of production which gratify bodily wants, whether simple or luxurious. Even the highest degree of animal comfort, therefore, seems but a paltry pittance to give to any industrious producer, out of the abundance of the age. Yet less than that is falling to the lot, to-day, of an actual majority of the toiling men and women

6

whose work has filled the world so full of riches
that they run to waste. Is this, do you think, a
necessary state of things? Is it a state of things
to be satisfied with?

"I have spoken of riches that run to waste out
of the abundance to which the world has attained.
You touched upon that point a little while ago, but
I did not think we were ready then to consider it.
We could not rightly estimate the wastefulness of
consumption until we had formed some idea of
the increase of production, as we have since done.
Let us now go back to it. You thought, you said,
that profligate and wasteful consumption, on the
part of those who are able to command possession
of the products of labor, cannot be restrained. I
do not quite agree with you. Can you tell me
what wasteful consumption is?"

I scratched my head and confessed that I did
not see how it could be defined with any precision
at all. "And that," I added, "constitutes just
the difficulty in the matter which I was setting before you."

"It is a difficulty," returned the judge, "and
I certainly would not undertake to draw a complete line between wasteful and unwasteful consumption. It cannot possibly be done. But I
have at least one very well defined notion on the
subject. Let us rid ourselves, first, of the confusion which the idea of "profligacy" introduces.

Profligate consumption is not necessarily wasteful consumption, in the economical sense. Profligacy is a word of shifting signification. It means differently to different persons and under different circumstances. That which seems profligate to one is not profligate to another, and it was this fact, I think, which you had mostly in mind, when you questioned the possibility of bringing the consumption of the products of labor under any controlling laws. But there is one broad law that can be laid down and which is sufficient, in the economical view, to cover the whole ground. It is this : that nothing can be said to be wasted which contributes to the gratifying or the satisfying of any taste or any want in man, whether natural or cultivated. From the moral standpoint this looks like a startlingly broad rule, but I am convinced that it represents the only view which political economy can take. We can make no distinction between true tastes and false tastes, or between vicious desires and virtuous ones, because we cannot agree about them. We can take account of no wastefulness in any consumption of labor which has distinctly an object in any human taste or human want. There *is* wastefulness, to be sure, because everything expended upon an unworthy object, or expended disproportionately to the importance of the object, is wasted ; but we simply cannot take account of it.

" Where, then, is the waste that we *can* take account of? I will tell you. It is in the consumption of wealth which has *no* object outside of itself. It is in that consumption of labor and of the products of labor which is for the sake of consumption only; which is for the sake, in other words, of displaying the ability to consume and which consumes objectlessly for that purpose. It is that which we call the ostentation of wealth, or of the power of consumption which wealth gives. This is the great robber of society. It steals more out of what belongs to the race at large, for the comforting and beautifying and enlarging of human life, than all the robber appetites and passions and vices put together. It is appalling to think of the extent to which it recklessly and with brutal insensateness destroys the common benefit that ought to accrue to mankind from the great inventions by which the fruitfulness of labor is multiplied. Look at one instance out of hundreds, which our lady-friends here can appreciate. The sewing-machine made it possible to cheapen enormously the construction of clothing and to set free from that work a vast quantity of labor for other fields of production, tributary to the conveniences of living, or to the sense of beauty, or to the desire for knowledge. Has it realized such a result, in any degree commensurate at all with what it added to the efficiency of labor in the employment of sewing? No. And why? Because a despicable, senseless, and most vulgar vanity in that minor fraction of mankind which has the power, more or less, to command labor at will, refuses to let clothing be cheapened, and persists in the contemptible display of an ability to possess and to wear clothes which cost much labor. So the 'world of fashion,' as we call it, exerts a perverted ingenuity in contriving forms of construction and frivolous changes in dress which shall constantly use up, and more than use up, if possible, all the gain to labor that is derived from mechanical invention. With what object? To improve our dress in durability or comfortableness? No. To add any quality of beauty, or gracefulness, or picturesqueness? No. To satisfy any demand from any kind of taste, whether pure and artistic or false? No. If these objects are thought of at all, they are the last and the least things considered in the edicts of fashion, to which a surviving barbarism in society is servile. It is a case of consumption, for the most part, with no object; of consumption for the sake of consuming, alone; of consumption to ostentate the power to consume. Am I not right?"

"You are," said my wife, " ' 'tis true, and pity 'tis 'tis true.' "

"The same is true," continued the judge, " of consumption in many other ways, to a monstrous extent. I think sometimes that almost half of what is expended among wealthy people upon their houses and the appurtenances of their living is expended only to measure against one another the expending power which they severally possess. There is not a desire, nor a taste, nor a sentiment, nor an emotion, nor even an animal sensation of the lowest kind, which prompts it or is gratified by it. It is simply an objectless consumption.

" Now, all this is barbaric and vulgar. It is of the essence of vulgarity. It is opposed to all the influences under which human character is being developed in the process of what we call civilization. It is offensive, as much to the practical common-sense, and to the bare, bald, calculating utilitarianism of habit, which grow with the growth of intelligence and faculty, as it is offensive to the finer instincts and perceptions that grow in the same process. Will you tell me that there is no hope of the evolution of a state of sentiment in society which will put checks upon this objectless, ostentatious consumption, by holding it in derision and contempt, thus destroying the one small, mean motive behind it and making it abortive? I believe differently. I know that there is a quicker sensitiveness in mankind to imputations of vulgarity than to imputations of immorality. I know that it is easier to attach social disgrace to the doings of things which impugn the polite culture of men than to the doing of things which impugn their virtue or their honesty. I know, therefore, that the poverty of taste, the poverty of resource, the poverty of capacity for enjoyment, which exhibit themselves in an aimless, ostentatious consumption of wealth, will become contemptible and ridiculous in our society long before the vices of appetite and taste which consume wealth unworthily and sinfully are disgraced and condemned. I have hope of seeing, even before my days are ended, the coming of the time when a great house, built for no uses of hospitality—a great house of closed chambers—a great house full of splendors out of which the possessor enjoys nothing except the poor consciousness of possession—will be looked upon as the monument of a barbarian who has survived beyond his age. Yet I have no hope of seeing in my time the extermination of immoral profligacy. Such is the difference of controllability, in my view, between the two kinds of wasteful consumption.

"And it ought to be so. Any robust, positive vice, out of which grow evil appetites and pernicious desires, is more tolerable than the nothingness of ostentation, as a consumer of the wealth of the world. I would have this preached as the gospel of social economy, until society is taught to exact from its members *some* account of their consumption of the products of its labor; whether morally satisfactory or not—whether æsthetically satisfactory or not—whether sensually satisfactory or not; exacting, simply, that there shall be objects of desire of some kind to account for their consumption. The world needs nothing nearer to communism than that. It has enough to afford to every man the gratification of all wants, all desires, and all tastes, that he can make himself capable of deriving enjoyment from, either by cultivation or by vitiation—no matter what their nature or their extravagance may be—if he will only make these the measure of his consumption and not consume aimlessly and wantonly beyond them."

The judge paused, and I said to him : " What then ? You have satisfied me that there may be some restraint put upon the wanton waste of wealth in ostentatious consumption, by vulgarizing it in public opinion; but what then ? You will only have changed the direction of expenditure, and stimulated the cultivation of wants and desires to absorb that which was consumed without desire before."

" Not so," he replied. " In the nature and in the cultivation of every man there are limits to the consumption of wealth which can yield enjoyment to him, if you suppress ostentation, or that which the keen perceptions of his fellows will detect as pretension and ostentation. And this is especially true of those men who make the acquisition of

wealth an end in life. They leave themselves little time for the cultivation of large tastes, large
desires or large capacities for personal enjoyment
of any kind. Not only that, but the natural tastes
and desires in them lose their edge. There is one
passion only in them that can make boundless demands upon wealth for its gratification, and that is
the love of power. But wealth yields power to the
possessor of it within limits that are very narrow
if it is not productively used, as by the Rothschilds
and the Vanderbilts, instead of being wastefully
consumed. As you discourage among men, therefore, the vain showing of wealth, by making that
vulgar and despicable, you drive them into finding
potent uses for it, and thus you throw a vast part
of what had been wastefully consumed, by barbaric ostentation, into the fund of productive capital. Is not that so?"

I was forced to assent.

"We have gone far enough, then, for to-night,"
said the judge. "We set out to discover how, and
from what sources, the fund of capital is susceptible of an increase that will enlarge the dividends
to productive labor, without disturbing the social
organization in which wealth is unequally distributed, and without impairing the inducements
to the accumulation of wealth. I think that I
have partly, though not wholly yet, answered your
questions on this point. We have seen what room

for such an increase is made by mechanical multi-
plications of the productiveness of labor, and by
the relative diminution of animals which compete
with man for subsistence from the earth, and you
have agreed with me that it is possible to cultivate
a state of feeling in society which will restrain
that kind of unproductive consumption that wastes
wealth in the empty ostentation of it. Let us
leave the matter here till to-morrow evening, and
then we will take up the 'wages-fund' in the
light of these facts."

So we parted for the night.

FIFTH EVENING.

ABOUT THE WAYS AND MEANS OF JUSTICE.

The "Wages - Fund" and the Wages System. — The Common "Compensation Fund" which may be substituted in Political Economy.—Effects of Partnership between Labor and Capital. — Its Practicable Beginnings and its Ultimate Consequences.—Loanable Capital and Public Debts.—The Judge's New Party.—Malthus and the Far Future.

"Now," said the judge, when we were seated together again, "let us try, if we can, to reach the end of our discussion to-night, for I am afraid that it is growing tiresome. We have got the way pretty well cleared before us, and ought to go over the remaining ground more rapidly.

"I do not pretend, you understand, to have the solution of this great labor-question formulated in any social theory. I do not pretend to lay down a scheme of doctrine for any school or any party of social reform. I am only trying to discover the facts which underlie the problem and the principles which bear upon it, and to contribute, if I can, some help toward opening it to proper study.

I know that it is not a subject for legislation, either in parliaments or in parties, nor a thing to be arbitrarily dealt with in any way. There are no solvents for it unless we can find them in public opinion, and my hope is in the appeal to that. I want to see given to the question the moral aspects which belong to it, along with the economical ones, holding the two together so that their modification of one another may be seen. It has been looked at too long from the opposite standpoints of the philanthropist and the political economist. I would like, if I can, to study it with the eyes of both; to clearly take in the hard environment of view to which political economy is restricted, and yet to do so without standing quite down at the level of dead facts, but lifted just so far into the region of sentiment that I may possibly see something behind and beyond, and find if there are moral forces lying latent there which may be capable of ameliorating that environment of hard conditions.

"I am convinced that there are such forces, and that they may be brought into gradual activity by a steady propagation of just notions in society concerning labor and capital, and concerning the acquisition and consumption and use of wealth. Not in the spirit of ranting demagoguism, nor of fanatical, unreasoning philanthropy, so called, but in the spirit of rational justice and of that practical, every-day common-sense in mankind which is becoming all-powerful.

"The doctrine of the 'wages-fund' in political economy rests solidly upon stubborn facts. But let us look at the nature of the facts. 'Wages,' says Mr. John Stuart Mill, 'not only depend upon the relative amount of capital and population, but cannot, under the rule of competition, be affected by anything else. Wages (meaning, of course, the general rate) cannot rise but by an increase of the aggregate funds employed in hiring laborers, or a diminution in the number of competitors for hire; nor fall except either by a diminution of the funds devoted to paying labor, or by an increase of the number of laborers to be paid.' Now, this is true —unquestionably true. But what then? We are not compelled to assume, as the political economists incline to do, that there is no possibility of forcing a relative increase of the aggregate funds employed in production. We might have to assume that, if we could find no sources from which to derive such an increase of the fund of capital, without interfering with the ordinary springs and motives of human action. If it could not be had without curtailing the gratification of wants and desires and tastes, on the part of those who command at will the consumption of labor and its products, we could not reasonably argue upon any other assumption. But we have found differently.

We have found that the augmented productiveness
of labor, since mechanical invention became active, actually outruns the desires of that minority
in society which has so far monopolized most of
the benefit from it, and that there is a sickening
wastefulness of consumption without object going
on, which is plainly susceptible of being restrained
by the influences that are developed in the progress of human culture.   In contemplating these
influences as available forces in social economy
we contemplate no opposition to human nature,
but are strictly in consonance with it.   We have
a right then, I say, to assume that some relative
increment of the aggregate fund of wealth appropriated to productive labor *is* possible, and we
have no right to assume the contrary.

   "Now comes the question, ' How can constraint
be brought upon those who hold possession of
wealth, to compel them to add more of it year by
year to the capital-fund, instead of consuming it ?'
Well, it cannot be done under the existing ' wages
system.' The political economists are right in
that. So long as the pay of the working-man continues to be a fixed quantity, it will continue to
be very near the lowest quantity at which equilibrium is established between his necessities and
the gainful desires of the man of wealth who employs him. So long as the capitalists think it right
to hold and use their dictatorial power in produc-

tion, and the working-man is nothing more than one troublesome factor out of several in their productive calculations, it is certain that the figures˙ which represent him in the calculation are not likely to change much in his favor. The x which stands for quantity of capital to be appropriated to production will bear a pretty constant ratio to the y which stands for quantity of dependent labor, divided by the z which represents the degree to which it is dependent. But change the relationship of the laborer to the capitalist, from that of hire to that of partnership—no matter by how slight an alteration—and see how the formula of the calculation is changed! He escapes at once from under the rule-of-three by which you settled wages for him. He is no longer a factor in the simple division of your 'wages-fund;' you have to reckon him now among the primary factors in the general division of the general product of labor. He has acquired what he did not have before—a certain proprietary interest in the aggregate fund of produced wealth, and has to be accounted to for his interest before the question, as to how much of what has been produced this year shall be dedicated to production next year, becomes an open question at all. He has acquired his suffrage, so to speak, in the matter of the allotment to be made between productive and unproductive consumption.

"We can see this plainly enough in an individual case, and can see with what effect it operates to modify the conditions of the distribution of the products of labor and to change the terms of the daily or yearly appropriation made out of them to the capital fund. Here is our young friend John, for example, receiving wages, I believe—or a salary, if that sounds better—from his employers. He is paid for his work a fixed compensation, which is chiefly determined by the existing demand for, and supply of, such services as he is qualified to perform. He draws it from what Mr. Mill calls 'the fund employed in hiring labor,' and there are limitations put upon it by the limits of that fund. But suppose that next year his employers, who think highly of him and feel friendly toward him, and who desire to attach him permanently in interest to themselves, admit him to a junior partnership in the concern, turning over to him a certain minor share of their property and business, which he is to pay for, perhaps, out of the earnings. He will have ceased then, will he not, to draw his remuneration for work out of the 'wages-fund?' He will have ceased to participate in that drawing of fixed shares from the aggregate product of labor which we call wages-paying, and will have become a participant in the division of that indefinite remainder out of which the appropriations to capital have chiefly to be made. He will have become, therefore, an absolute instead of a relative factor in the division of the product. He will have been lifted out of dependence upon the 'wages-fund,' into a relationship toward the whole fund of produced wealth which is potentially independent; and that will have been a great gain for Master John, even though his dividends from the earnings of the business should be no greater than his wages are now.

"He will have owed it, too, to a generous concession on the part of his employers; that is, if he has no capital to put into their business equivalent to the partnership in it which they concede to him. No doubt they will have been actuated by considerable motives of self-interest in the matter. No doubt they will have expected to gain some relief from care and exertion for themselves, and to gain some energy in the prosecution and management of their business, by infusing young blood into the proprietorship. But still there will have been a strong element of magnanimity in the concession. They are under no necessity to make it, and if they are men of mean selfishness they will not make it. They will try, on the contrary, to retain John's services under hire as long as they can, and then, when he will work for wages no longer, to find some one else of like capacity and fidelity, but more dependent than he, to take his place. They prefer, however, as we suppose, to unite John permanently in interest with themselves, and it is with motives partly selfish and partly generous that they open the door for him through which he steps to the more independent footing of a proprietary producer, and passes at once outside of the domain of your inexorable law of the 'wages-fund,' because he becomes then one of the administrators of the law.

"Now, suppose that these same employers should be further induced by like considerations to make the same kind of concession, in some small way, to every other man·in their employ, turning over to him, on the same terms, some little share of interest in their establishment—no matter how little—or supplementing his wages by some slight fraction of dividend from the profits of the business—no matter how slight; would they not, then, have done for him, proportionately, the same thing which they had done for Master John, and made the like change in his relations to production and capital? Would they not, to that extent, have abrogated in their establishment the law of the 'wages-fund,' and introduced another law, to which the appropriations made from production to capital would have to conform to themselves?

" And, then, suppose that all the employers in the country should be induced to do the same

thing ! What would have happened ? Why, your
'wages-fund' would have disappeared out of the
calculations of political economy, because it would
have ceased to be a definable fund. We could as
well talk of a 'profit-fund,' and there is certainly
no such thing as that, in any definable sense; because the profits of capital are simply that remainder of the product of labor which is left in its
possession, after giving to the producing laborers
just what the competition of their necessities will
compel them to accept. In the case supposed, we
should have merged the whole together in one
common 'compensation-fund.' With what result ?
Simply this : our present wages system establishes
a given set of conditions, to which production has
to be conformed, and there is reserved from consumption for renewed production just such a fund
of capital as those conditions exact. If we introduced the new set of conditions which the system
of dividends contemplates, they would be just as
arbitrary and compulsory ; production would have
to be adapted to them, and the reserve for capital
would again be precisely what they exact. It
could not be otherwise."

" But that involves, does it not," said I, " a reduction of the profits of capital corresponding to
the addition made to the remuneration of labor ? "

" No, not a corresponding reduction," returned
the judge. " No doubt it involves some encroach-

ment upon the general rate of profit which capital
now enjoys and is habituated to expect, but not to
the extent that might be feared. The greater part
of the gain to the working-man will ultimately be
an absolute and clear gain, costing the capitalist
nothing. The provision for it will be found in an
increase of product, relatively to the capital. employed, resulting from the stimulation of labor by
more animating. and energetic motives. We can
certainly calculate upon that, and largely, because
we know what self-interest is worth as a stimulant
of human exertion. The most conscientious man
is incapable, as a rule, of constantly doing quite
his best in work when the personal benefit to himself from it is not affected by small differences of
industry and carefulness and watchful attention.
He may try to exert himself for another with the
same faithfulness and energy and zeal that he
would for himself, but he cannot always do it.
He is betrayed into relaxations of spirit which he
is not conscious of. Although he does not feel it
or know it, there is the want in him of one elastic
spring of action that would keep the moral motives of his work at a steadier tension. It' is the
knowledge of this fact in human nature that chiefly
induces employers of labor to do that which we
supposed in the case of our young friend John.
By admitting a faithful employé into partnership,
or by holding out that prospect to him, they cal-.

culate upon enlisting a new motor in him that will reënforce the motives of conscience and add energy to his whole performance of service. And the calculation rarely fails.

"Now, I am sure that the same effect will follow the widest application of the experiment. But it will not be an instantaneous effect. It will follow very slowly, perhaps, and the experiment that I refer to cannot be otherwise than a tentative and gradual one, to be successful. I should not dream of having it entered upon by any sudden and universal movement, if that were possible, because I know that it would fail. I have said already that the dependent laboring-class, as a body, needs to be educated for it, by slow and careful beginnings in the introduction of the new system. It is inevitable that much of the introductory experimenting will be abortive; but that offers no discouragement, if we convince ourselves that the direction taken is right. My wish is only to see a movement in the interest of the laboring-people set in that right direction, no matter how slow it may be. That such a work of reform must begin with a work of education on the part of those who are to benefit by it, we can readily see. One of the main elements of the force to be generated in labor, by setting independent personal interests and personal prospects before it, is that of ambition or aspiration. But there are a great many laborers, of the duller sort, who are obviously not capable of feeling ambitious. There are no sufficient aspirations to be awakened in them. There is an inheritance in them,' perhaps, of natures blunted through many generations by hard conditions of life. There are many others who may be capable of ambitious sentiments, but who are not capable of the provident fore-calculation, or the postponement of desires to anticipations and the sacrifice of present ease for future enjoyment, which effective ambition involves. These large classes are almost hopelessly doomed to the conditions of the present labor system. It will be long generations, no doubt, before they can be effectively acted upon by any stimulant of opportunity that may be given them. But it is needless, meantime, that all the rest of the great brotherhood of labor should be doomed by the incapacity of these. It is not necessary that the leaden weight of one stolid part should be laid on the whole class to hold it down. Why not set that kind of a system on foot which shall sift out the enterprising from the inert and distinguish those who are capable of laying hold of better opportunities in life from those who are not? Then trust that emulation and example and encouragement and hope will work like a slow leaven through the whole heavy mass.

"If I made any proposition on the subject, I

should propose that, for the beginning of the experiment of dividends to labor, it be based altogether upon the expectation of an increased product, relatively to capital employed, and be carried only so far as that expectation may be realized. In other words, that the employers of labor be persuaded to begin to say to their employed laborers this: 'We are deriving, now, a certain rate of profit—say the average of past years—from the business in which our capital, our exertions in management, and your labor, are engaged together. This is the compensation which seems to be fixed for us by the conditions of the present system of simple wages-paying. We are accustomed to it, and we are not willing either to exert ourselves or to expose our capital to commercial risks for less. But if you will make the rate of profit greater, by working with more energy and more efficiency; by using our tools, our materials, and our capital in general more economically, and by giving more careful attention to all the interests in which you are concerned with us, we will divide the whole increase of profit so produced among you, proportionately, as near as may be, to what you have severally contributed to it. We will take to ourselves, in other words, no more than the remuneration that we have been accustomed to, and all beyond that shall be yours. We will pay you wages in the mean time, as heretofore, according to

the market.   If we find some among you who are
making exertions to give effect to this proposition
and others who are not, we shall not permit the
latter to steal the benefit of the exertions of the
former.   We shall get rid of them as soon as possible.   We shall try to find men to take their
places who will coöperate with their fellows and
with us in this experiment, or else we shall try, in
conjunction with the better workmen, to adjust a
scale of wages, or a system of piece-work, in which
the relative value of the labor of each workman
shall be fairly measured, to determine his share of
the proposed dividend.'

"Now, I have no doubt that this might be tried
with good effect to the working-men, and not only
with no risk, but with much benefit, to the employing capitalists.   I have no doubt that those who
adopted it would find themselves placed at an advantage in competition with those who did not.
They would win to themselves the best workmen;
their business would be more easily conducted and
extended, and its management would impose upon
them less care and less exertion.   Nor have I any
doubt that the beginning of such a movement on
the side of the employers would be responded to
very quickly on the side of the better and more
ambitious working-men, by a movement toward
raising the standard of character and workmanship in their several trades, and toward combining

individualism with coöperation. They would be prompted to throw their influence against that fatal policy in the trades-unions which establishes a mean level of mediocrity and shiftlessness, which represses ambition, crushes personal freedom, and wears out all the energies there are in the struggle that labor makes for better conditions, by harnessing them to dead loads of incapability and laziness. They would exert themselves to make the trade-union what it might be—the organized government of a craft; powerful to maintain justice and liberty among its members; to secure for each the largest exercise of his capabilities; to stimulate in each the highest ambition; to dignify to every one the estimate of his avocation; to fix just standards of qualification and obligation, and to enforce just rules of apprenticeship, despising every other attempt than that to narrow the doors of admission to any trade. I believe, as I live, that such results as these would follow, and I do not believe that the blind mischief which the labor-unions of the present time are doing, both to labor and capital, can be arrested in any other way than by the invitation and encouragement of something different from an unmixed wages system. What do you think?"

"It looks reasonable," said I. "It *is* reasonable. I cannot see the least room for doubting that you are right. But, if nothing beyond pres-

7

ent wages is to be distributable among the laborers except just the increase of product to which
their labor may be stimulated, the gain to them,
although considerable, cannot be all that final
equity, in your view, demands. According to
what you have said, you evidently contemplate
something more in the end."

"Oh, yes," was his reply; "we must not disguise the fact that ultimately something more is
involved, if we once introduce the principle of dividends to labor, and give recognition to it on even
the smallest scale. There is no question in my
mind that it will finally involve a considerable reduction of the profits of capital. The pressure of
the principle, systematically organized, will steadily force them down. But it is very plain to me
that there is ample room for such a reduction of
profits, from their present average rate, as will afford all the addition that is needful and just to the
compensations of labor, without impairing at all
the strength of the motives on which the accumulation and employment of capital depend. Let us
look at them:

"The payment which the employing capitalist
demands from the production to which his capital
is applied is made up of three parts. There is—
1. The payment to him for having refrained, during successive years, from the entire consumption
of his acquisitions of wealth, and for having saved

and accumulated them and employed them productively—which Mr. Senior has happily called
'the remuneration of abstinence.' There is—2.
The payment to him for risks of loss, which are
taken in nearly all employments of capital, owing
to the casualties and uncertainties of production
and trade. There is—3. The payment to him,
when he is the manager of his own capital, for his
personal executive services in connection with it.

The first of these payments—that for the remuneration of abstinence—seems to diminish as
the state of civilization advances, as the accumulation of capital increases, and as the effective desire of accumulation is developed. That it is
capable of being reduced very low, without dis-
couraging the abstinence which augments capital,
we have good evidence in the world already. We
have an exact measure of it in the current rate of
interest on money that is loaned out upon such
security that no risk attends the loaning. Government loans, in countries where a state of political stability is well assured, are of that character.
The element of risk is so nearly eliminated from
such investments of capital that there is no need
of reckoning it at all. It is about the same with
safe loans on mortgage, and with some personal
investments, also, in property which cannot be impaired under any probable contingency. Now, the
rate of interest on permanent or prolonged loans

of the kind described has fallen in England and Holland to two and three per cent., and those are countries in which the motives that produce an accumulation of capital seem to be more energetic than in almost any others. This low rate of interest represents the minimum reward which will constitute, in those countries, a sufficient inducement to abstinence from the present consumption of wealth, and a sufficient encouragement, therefore, to that cumulative employment of labor which produces capital.

" As for the second ground of payment to capital, which is for the risk of its destruction, when employed as in manufactures or in trade, the hazards to which it is exposed are of two kinds. It may be absolutely destroyed and go out of existence, both as wealth and capital, by casualties of fire, flood, shipwreck, etc.; or, only the right of property which the investor had in it may be destroyed, through the vicissitudes of commerce, so that it passes into other hands, either to be unproductively consumed or to be still used as capital with a change of ownership merely. The value of the first-named class of risks has been found susceptible, for the most part, of very exact calculation, under the averaging law of chances, and it is set down in the rates of insurance. The capitalist almost always transfers that class of risks to those who have made a special business of taking them, and his payments for insurance are charged into the expenses of his own proper business, so that remuneration for these risks is no part, generally speaking, of the profit which he demands to compensate him for his employment of capital. The value of the risk, moreover, is slight—surprisingly slight, now that our underwriting arithmetic has reduced it to a precise computation. Of the second class of risks, the greater part are incident to the character and conduct of the investor of capital, and attach so entirely to himself that he has no fair reason for making a charge against the community on account of them. Not all of them, to be sure, for there are elements of uncertainty in production and trade which elude all forecalculation, and some liberal allowance is to be made for these; but it is unquestionably true that the investor of capital in productive or commercial enterprises risks far more upon his own knowledge, his own judgment, his own alertness of perception, his own economical vigilance, his own calculating faculties and his own prudence, than in any other way. I venture to say that seven-tenths, at least, of all the losses and failures that occur in the manufacturing and mercantile world are due to one or the other of the following causes, or to all of them combined: 1. The want of a sufficiently wide knowledge of the conditions of the business pursued, or inattention to the changes of the facts which bear upon it: 2. Miscalculation from the facts known, either through careless or incompetent reckoning. 3. Thriftless and wasteful management, due to the want of watchful executive force. 4. Ill-judged confidence in others—extending credit incautiously and unwisely. 5. Reckless speculation, or taking chances of the market which are illegitimate, because outside of the realm of rational calculation. 6. Last and greatest of all— personal extravagance, or personal consumption in excess of any reasonable reckoning of business profits. Now, these are all sources of risk which lie within the control of the investor of capital, and which cannot be properly charged for in the demand for profits upon capital invested and managed by the owner. The risks which lie outside are comparatively small.

"Finally, we have the payment to be made for the personal executive services of the capitalist and business manager. I am willing to put a liberal estimate upon these, but not to rate them extravagantly beyond the compensations paid for all other kinds of service. To the man of business, ordinarily, his business is his pleasure, its occupations his delight. He pursues it, ordinarily, even after the merely gainful desires have ceased to act with any strong stimulation upon him. He has no other sufficient field of activity open to him; he has no other sufficient resources of enjoyment. Without the occupations of his business he would be wretched. I am sure, therefore, that no extraordinary remuneration is needed to induce men of business faculties to employ their faculties, and I see no reason why their compensation for personal services should exceed, at most, the higher salaries paid in public and professional life.

"Looking, therefore, at all the parts of the payment made to the capitalist, in the form of profits, I conclude that there is room for a considerable reduction in their rate without weakening the inducements to abstinence, by which capital is accumulated, or weakening the inducement of risks in the employment of capital, or weakening the inducements to exertion in the management of capital. If the general introduction of a system of dividends to labor should result in the partitioning of something less than twenty or fifteen or even ten per cent. of the total product of labor to the business-managing capitalist for his profit, I am confident that the efficiency of the forces which political economy takes account of would not be at all impaired. The consequence of such a system would simply be, that the minimum measure of the inducements under which capital can be accumulated and employed would be found; and that would be the realization of justice between capital and labor."

" But, for the bringing about of this state of things," said I, " you look to nothing except the growths of public sentiment and opinion which you have alluded to, from time to time, in our discussion ? "

" To nothing else," he answered, " except in one direction. There is one direction, only, in which I would invoke the aid of legislation. To that single end I would make the question a political one, and, if I had in me any of the qualities of an agitator, I would go among the working-men and set up in their midst the standard of a new party, to be organized upon that solitary issue, and I would try to rally them about it until they had fought the issue out in every country under the sun. I would rally them, if I could, as a class, in uncompromising hostility to all public debt-making, of every kind, whether national or municipal. I would have them demand, and combine to enforce their demand, that the power to contract debt be absolutely taken away from every branch and division of government—from Congress and Parliament down—unless taxation to pay the debt, within three or five years at most, shall precede or go with the debt-making act. To accomplish that abolition of debt-making power in government would be the greatest triumph ever won in the interest of labor. I will tell you why.

" We have seen at what a multiplying rate production has increased during the past hundred years, and is increasing. We have seen, too, how easy it is, under the present system of things, for enormous accumulations of the wealth thus increasingly produced to be gathered into individual hands. Now, an always-growing share of these accumulations is held by owners who cannot or who do not wish to employ it productively themselves, although they are eager to preserve it as a profitable fund, unimpaired by their own consumption. This constitutes the loanable capital of the world, and its quantity, as I have said, is being prodigiously augmented. There is a fast-increasing number of men who hold more wealth, outside of their consumption, than they can possibly use productively under their own management; there is another fast-increasing number of men who desire to escape from the cares, exertions, and risks of the management of property productively employed; and, again, there is more and more inherited wealth existing, in estates, where it is so situated that, for one reason or another, it cannot be productively employed by the owners in person. All these people resort to the loaning of their wealth, at interest, as the means of making it productive of income to themselves without personal exertion, and of course they seek, in doing so, to avoid risks and to get the utmost security they can, either for the final replacement to them of the

wealth which they have given out of their own
keeping, or for the certainty and permanency of
the interest-payments that are to be made to them
for the use of it. There is no fault to be found
with this disposition on the part of the loaning
class, for it is natural and right; but it must not
be permitted to create artificially, for it own satisfaction, modes of investment or consumption of
wealth which are opposed to the interests of productive labor, and which lay lasting burdens upon
it. That, however, is just the effect that it has
been producing for the last hundred years and
more. The demand for opportunities to make safe
loans of unemployed wealth, or of money, as we
say, has forced the fearful growth, in later times,
of national and municipal debts. An incorporated
community, stably organized, is the most trust-
worthy of all debtors. Its pecuniary obligations
are a joint mortgage upon the property of all its
members. No individual borrower can offer se-
curities quite equal to that. Hence public loans,
in every country of a creditable character, have
been sought for with ravenous avidity. A fatal
facility in debt-making, on the part of all the corporate divisions of government, from that of the
State at large down to that of the smallest village
community, has been the consequence, and the
loaning class has exerted a strong pressure of in-
visible and hardly conscious influence in favor of

the making of debts. Thus public debts, both
national and municipal, have swollen, within the
last century, until their aggregate magnitude is
appalling to the political economist. They represent not only an outrageous mortgage upon future
production, but a more outrageous waste, in the
consumption of wealth which the owners would
not themselves consume, and which might have
been added to the productive capital of the world.
Three-quarters, at least, of all the borrowed wealth
which governments have consumed and which the
people are under bonds to account for, has simply
undergone destruction in their hands, by methods
of sheer wastefulness that are more wanton than
any other. It has been devoured by armies, or
has vanished in the smoke of battle, or it has been
squandered by a thousand modes in extravagant
and reckless administration. For some little part
of the vast total of public debt there are public
improvements of permanent usefulness to show—
such as edifices and roads and canals; but I doubt
if all these put together in the world will stand
for one-fourth of the whole. The stupendous remainder represents, for the greater part, a wicked
obliteration of wealth in one generation at the cost
of posterity.

"Now, I do not maintain that armies can yet
be dispensed with altogether in the world, nor that
war can be always averted; but I do say that the

fatal facility in borrowing which governments have
acquired, by reason of the productive progress of
the world, and through the fatal habit of indiffer-
ence to debt which is fostered by the pressure of
the increasing demand for public loans as an investment of idle wealth, are at the bottom of the causes
which produce in modern times oppressive mili-
tary establishments and ambitious wars. At the
same time, they are the underlying causes of corruption, extravagance, and recklessness in public
expenditure, wherever found, in State or municipal
government. It is so easy to make up a deficiency
in revenue by an issue of bonds, for which eager
lenders are always waiting, and public opinion is
easily reconciled to small accretions of a debt
that has outgrown the apprehension of its figures. The process is an utterly ruinous one, and
it must be arrested, in the interest of labor, from
whose use all this wealth, which might be working capital, is abstracted, on the one hand, to be
added, on the other, to the burden of a lasting
mortgage on the products of labor. It must be
arrested, peremptorily and absolutely. The working-class and the class of active capitalists must
combine their strength of numbers, in political
action, to put a stop to it, by constitutionally de-
priving all governments of the power to contract
debt, except in the temporary way that I have indicated. Some carefully-limited borrowing power

of that kind is undoubtedly necessary, to provide
for emergencies which cannot be forecalculated,
and it would suffice for all contingencies that are
conceivable. It would have sufficed amply in our
own case, when we were driven to war for the
preservation of the Union—and no people were
ever placed in a situation of greater stress. It
seemed to us at the time that we could not bear
the cost of so great a struggle in immediate taxation; but we can easily see now that it would have
been better for us if we had done so. It would
have been better if we had been left with no other
alternative. The Union was not worth saving to
us if we could have shrunk from the payment of
the cost then and there. As it was, by borrowing,
we imposed more than a double cost upon ourselves and our children and our children's children.
For every actual dollar's worth of wealth and labor
that we consumed in the prosecution of the war,
we laid a mortgage for more than two dollars on
the future production of the country, by reason of
the inflation of prices which resulted from the
forced loan of the legal-tender issue."

"Let me understand," said I, "exactly how
you would propose to limit the borrowing power
of government."

"I should not limit the *sum* which a government may borrow in situations of temporary emer-
gency, or for extraordinary purposes of importance,

because there is no ground of calculation to go
upon in fixing such a limit; but I should strictly
and severely narrow down the conditions under
which all public borrowing is to be done. I should
make it a matter of constitutional law, applying to
all the subdivisions of government, that every act
which authorizes a loan shall contain in itself the
provisions of extra taxation for paying the prin-
cipal of the loan within three or five years at the
most, and that such provisions of taxation shall be
subject to no repeal, nor to any modification which
impairs the revenue from them, after the loan shall
have been consummated. The effect would be to
make all public expenditure, whether ordinary or
extraordinary, immediately dependent upon the
temper and disposition of the tax-paying people,
as it ought to be. If the object of proposed expenditure be not urgent and important enough to
command their assent to immediate additional
taxes, it is proper that such expenditure should be
barred. Administrators and legislators would be
exposed to a more rigorous criticism, and held to a
stricter account of reasons for every appropriation
which exceeds the ordinary revenues of government. Extravagance would be checked, and recklessness in political schemes of personal ambition
as well, while the needful energies of government
would suffer no detriment, I am sure.

" You can see what consequences of advantage

to labor would accrue. The loanable wealth, which now finds investment in public loans, to the extent of many thousands of millions of dollars, would be driven to take the risks, more or less, of productive employment, and be added perforce to the working capital· of the world. The men who either cannot or will not undertake for themselves the productive employment of such funds as they desire income from, would be impelled to trust more of them than they now do to the use and management of those who will. · Industrial enterprise would be powerfully reënforced, and a vast improvement made in the conditions of labor at once."

"Well, judge," said I, "I will join your party. I can heartily subscribe to the one resolution of its platform. Let us begin with a party of two, and there is no telling what will come of it.

"As for the rest of the doctrines you have expounded to us, they are like the seeds of this apple that I have bitten, in which some far-off possible fruitage may be dimly discerned by those who have the vision of faith which you possess. They are very grand doctrines of justice; very inspiring doctrines of hopefulness; very noble in the conception of duty between man and man which they body forth, and very lofty in the ideal of human society which they set up. But there is only the potential seed of truth in them, as you admit yourself. Like the seed of this apple, they must be planted, and must wait in obscure darkness for the dull earth to feel them and to be felt by them; and they must be dissolved by its storms and heated by its fermentations, before any germ of vital force can make its appearance in them. Will you plant them? Will you put what you have said here into written words, which may be dropped along the highways and get their chance, at least, of germination in the thoughts and acts of other men?"

He shook his head. "I cannot," he said. "I found long ago that writing is not my province of work in the world. I have not the courage nor the ambition for such a task."

"Then I shall take the duty upon myself. I have been keeping a record of our talks, which is not very far from exact. If you do not prohibit me, I shall give it to print, because I think there are hints of teaching in it which ought to have some wider audience than this."

He only shrugged his shoulders and smiled, as he rose to depart, and the smile, which had no protest in it, is my warrant for the publication of our talks.

"Just one last question," I added, as he stood at the door.

"If there be a possible state of easy conditions in life for all working-men and working-women,

how long can it last before the world becomes pop-
ulated in excess of the sustaining capabilities of
its soil ? "

"Ah! that," said the judge, " is a question that
we must leave with God. Malthus has not troubled
me at all, although I do not forget him. The
laws of increase in population which he deduced
are beyond dispute, but it is horrible to construe
them as oracles of doom against any wretched class
of human creatures. I find, for my own part, no
argument of hopelessness in them. It is certain
that the checks upon population which are found
in prudent restraints of marriage, act, in the several classes of society, with a strength somewhat
proportioned to the culture and experience of the
class. It is in the state of poverty, not of wealth,
that the fecundity of the race increases. It is
among the poor that marriage is earliest and most
improvident; it is among the poor that marriage
is the most fruitful. On the other hand, perhaps,
it is in the ranks of the pinched and degraded poor
that death works busiest to cut the increase down;
but shall we dare to found cold calculations on that?
I dare not, for one.

"As for the final end to which your question
looks—it is beyond our ken. We must trust it
where we trust all that belongs to the final destiny
of the human race. It lies far off as yet—much
farther than it seemed to do when Malthus wrote.

We are finding out ways to produce more and more. We are producing with less dependence on the brutes which compete with man for subsistence from the earth. We may learn by and by to consume with less waste. The old local boundaries of subsistence are fast breaking down. Men are held no longer, as they were, to the spot of earth on which they were born. America has been opened for the discharge of population from Europe, and Africa will open wide doors in the near future. It will be long before the world is full of people and its soil can feed no more. Ere that time comes, man may possibly have learned to make food from the inorganic elements for himself. Who knows? It will be as God has willed. Let us leave the matter with him."

THE END.

INTERNATIONAL SCIENTIFIC SERIES.

NOW READY.

No. 1. FORMS OF WATER, in Clouds, Rain, Rivers, Ice, and Glaciers. By Prof. JOHN TYNDALL, LL. D., F. R. S. 1 vol. Cloth. Price, $1.50.

No. 2. PHYSICS AND POLITICS; or, Thoughts on the Application of the Principles of "Natural Selection" and "Inheritance" to Political Society. By WALTER BAGEHOT, Esq., author of "The English Constitution." 1 vol. Cloth. Price, $1.50.

No. 3. FOODS. By EDWARD SMITH, M. D., LL. B., F. R. S. 1 vol. Cloth. Price, $1.75.

No. 4. MIND AND BODY. The Theories of their Relation. By ALEX. BAIN, LL. D., Professor of Logic in the University of Aberdeen. 1 vol., 12mo. Cloth. Price, $1.50.

No. 5. THE STUDY OF SOCIOLOGY. By HERBERT SPENCER. Price, $1.50.

No. 6. THE NEW CHEMISTRY. By Prof. JOSIAH P. COOKE, Jr., of Harvard University. 1 vol., 12mo. Cloth. Price, $2.00.

No. 7. THE CONSERVATION OF ENERGY. By Prof. BALFOUR STEWART, LL. D., F. R. S. 1 vol., 12mo. Cloth. Price, $1.50.

No. 8. ANIMAL LOCOMOTION; or, Walking, Swimming, and Flying, with a Dissertation on Aëronautics. By J. BELL PETTIGREW, M. D., F. R. S., F. R. S. E., F. R. C. P. E. 1 vol., 12mo. Fully illustrated. Price, $1.75.

No. 9. RESPONSIBILITY IN MENTAL DISEASE. By HENRY MAUDSLEY, M. D. 1 vol., 12mo. Cloth. Price, $1.50.

No. 10. THE SCIENCE OF LAW. By Prof. SHELDON AMOS. 1 vol., 12mo. Cloth. Price, $1.75.

No. 11. ANIMAL MECHANISM. A Treatise on Terrestrial and Aërial Locomotion. By E. J. MAREY. With 117 Illustrations. Price, $1.75.

No. 12. THE HISTORY OF THE CONFLICT BETWEEN RELIGION AND SCIENCE. By JOHN WM. DRAPER, M. D., LL. D., author of "The Intellectual Development of Europe." Price, $1.75.

No. 13. THE DOCTRINE OF DESCENT AND DARWINISM. By Prof. OSCAR SCHMIDT, Strasburg University. Price, $1.50.

No. 14. THE CHEMISTRY OF LIGHT AND PHOTOGRAPHY. In its Application to Art, Science, and Industry. By Dr. HERMANN VOGEL. 100 Illustrations. Price, $2.00.

No. 15. FUNGI; their Nature, Influence, and Uses. By M. C. COOKE, M. A., LL. D. Edited by Rev. M. J. BERKELEY, M. A., F. L. S. With 109 Illustrations. Price, $1.50.

No. 16. THE LIFE AND GROWTH OF LANGUAGE. By Prof. W. D. WHITNEY, of Yale College. Price, $1.50.

No. 17. MONEY AND THE MECHANISM OF EXCHANGE. By W. STANLEY JEVONS, M. A., F. R. S., Professor of Logic and Political Economy in the Owens College, Manchester. Price, $1.75.

No. 18. THE NATURE OF LIGHT, with a General Account of Physical Optics. By Dr. EUGENE LOMMEL, Professor of Physics in the University of Erlangen. With 188 Illustrations and a Plate of Spectra in Chromolithography. Price, $2.00.

No. 19. ANIMAL PARASITES AND MESSMATES. By Monsieur VAN BENEDEN, Professor of the University of Louvain, Correspondent of the Institute of France. With 83 Illustrations. Price, $1.50.

No. 20. ON FERMENTATIONS. By P. SCHÜTZENBERGER, Director at the Chemical Laboratory at the Sorbonne. With 28 Illustrations. Price, $1.50.

No. 21. THE FIVE SENSES OF MAN.

D. APPLETON & CO., PUBLISHERS, 549 & 551 Broadway, N. Y.

THE INTERNATIONAL SCIENTIFIC SERIES.

D. APPLETON & CO. have the pleasure of announcing that they have made arrangements for publishing, and have recently commenced the issue of, a SERIES OF POPULAR MONOGRAPHS, or small works, under the above title, which will embody the results of recent inquiry in the most interesting departments of advancing science.

The character and scope of this series will be best indicated by a reference to the names and subjects included in the subjoined list, from which it will be seen that the coöperation of the most distinguished professors in England, Germany, France, and the United States, has been secured, and negotiations are pending for contributions from other eminent scientific writers.

The works will be issued in New York, London, Paris, Leipsic, Milan, and St. Petersburg.

The INTERNATIONAL SCIENTIFIC SERIES is entirely an American project, and was originated and organized by Dr. E. L. Youmans, who has spent much time in Europe, arranging with authors and publishers.

FORTHCOMING VOLUMES.

Prof. W. KINGDON CLIFFORD, M. A. *The First Principles of the Exact Sciences explained to the Non-mathematical.*

Prof. T. H. HUXLEY, LL. D., F. R. S. *Bodily Motion and Consciousness.*

Dr. W. B. CARPENTER, LL. D., F. R. S. *The Physical Geography of the Sea.*

Prof. WILLIAM ODLING, F. R. S. *The Old Chemistry viewed from the New Stand-point.*

W. LAUDER LINDSAY, M. D., F. R. S. E. *Mind in the Lower Animals.*

Sir JOHN LUBBOCK, Bart., F. R. S. *On Ants and Bees.*

Prof. W. T. THISELTON DYER, B. A., B. Sc. *Form and Habit in Flowering Plants.*

Mr. J. N. LOCKYER, F. R. S. *Spectrum Analysis.*

Prof. MICHAEL FOSTER, M. D. *Protoplasm and the Cell Theory.*

H. CHARLTON BASTIAN, M. D., F. R. S. *The Brain as an Organ of Mind.*

Prof. A. C. RAMSAY, LL. D., F. R. S. *Earth Sculpture: Hills, Valleys, Mountains, Plains, Rivers, Lakes; How they were Produced, and how they have been Destroyed.*

Prof. RUDOLPH VIRCHOW (Berlin University). *Morbid Physiological Action.*

Prof. CLAUDE BERNARD. *History of the Theories of Life.*

D. APPLETON & CO., PUBLISHERS, 549 & 551 Broadway, N. Y.

THE INTERNATIONAL SCIENTIFIC SERIES.

FORTHCOMING VOLUMES.

Prof. H. SAINTE-CLAIRE DEVILLE. *An Introduction to General Chemistry.*

Prof. WURTZ. *Atoms and the Atomic Theory.*

Prof. De QUATREFAGES. *The Human Race.*

Prof. LACAZE-DUTHIERS. *Zoölogy since Cuvier.*

Prof. BERTHELOT. *Chemical Synthesis.*

Prof. C. A. YOUNG, Ph. D. (of Dartmouth College). *The Sun.*

Prof. OGDEN N. ROOD (Columbia College, N. Y.). *Modern Chromatics and its Relations to Art and Industry.*

Prof. J. ROSENTHAL. *General Physiology of Muscles and Nerves.*

Prof. JAMES D. DANA, M. A., LL. D. *On Cephalization ; or, Head-characters in the Gradation and Progress of Life.*

Prof. S. W. JOHNSON, M. A. *On the Nutrition of Plants.*

Prof. AUSTIN FLINT, Jr., M. D. *The Nervous System, and its Relation to the Bodily Functions.*

Prof. FERDINAND COHN (Breslau University). *Thallophytes (Algæ, Lichens, Fungi)*.

Prof. HERMANN (University of Zurich). *Respiration.*

Prof. LEUCKART (University of Leipsic). *Outlines of Animal Organization.*

Prof. LIEBREICH (University of Berlin). *Outlines of Toxicology.*

Prof. KUNDT (University of Strasburg). *On Sound.*

Prof. REES (University of Erlangen). *On Parasitic Plants.*

Prof. STEINTHAL (University of Berlin). *Outlines of the Science of Language.*

P. BERT (Professor of Physiology, Paris). *Forms of Life and other Cosmical Conditions.*

E. ALGLAVE (Professor of Constitutional and Administrative Law at Douai, and of Political Economy at Lille). *The Primitive Elements of Political Constitutions.*

P. LORAIN (Professor of Medicine, Paris). *Modern Epidemics.*

Mons. FREIDEL. *The Functions of Organic Chemistry.*

Mons. DEBRAY. *Precious Metals.*

Prof. CORFIELD, M. A., M. D. (Oxon.). *Air in its Relation to Health.*

Prof. A. GIARD. *General Embryology.*

D. APPLETON & CO., PUBLISHERS, 549 & 551 Broadway, N. Y.

RECENT PUBLICATIONS.

Diseases of Modern Life. By Dr. B. W. RICHARDSON, F. R. S. 1 vol., 12mo. Cloth. $2.00.

"' Diseases of Modern Life' is a work which throws so much light on what it is of the utmost importance for the public to know, that it deserves to be thoroughly and generally read."—*Graphic.*

'The literature on preventive medicine has received no more valuable contribution than this admirably-written treatise by one of the most accomplished physicians of Great Britain, who has concentrated upon his task a great amount of scientific research and clinical experience. No book that we have ever read more fully merits the attention of the intelligent public, to whom it is addressed."—*The World.*

Comin' Thro' the Rye. 1 vol., 8vo. Paper covers. 75 cents.

"A very amusing and well-written story. The history of the youth of the Adairs is extremely amusing, and told in a bright and witty manner. . . . One of the pleasantest novels of the season."—*Morning Post.*

"It is a clever novel, never dull, and the story never hangs fire."—*Standard.*

Memoir and Correspondence of Caroline Herschel. By Mrs. JOHN HERSCHEL. With Portraits. 12mo. Cloth. $1.75.

"The unlimited admiration excited by the noble, heroic virtues, and the uncommon talents of the subject of the memoir, is overborne by the intense sympathy felt for her long life of unselfish and unregretted devotion to others."—*Chicago Tribune.*

General History of Greece, from the Earliest Period to the Death of Alexander the Great. By the Rev. GEORGE W. COX. 1 vol., 12mo. Cloth. $2.50.

"We envy those schoolboys and undergraduates who will make their first acquaintance with Greek history through Mr. Cox's admirable volume. It ought to supersede all the popular Histories of Greece which have gone before it."—*The Hour.*

"The book is worthy, in every way, of the author's reputation. . . . It is altogether a most interesting and valuable book."—*Educational Times.*

A Short History of Natural Science and of the Progress of Discovery from the Time of the Greeks to the Present Day. By ARABELLA B. BUCKLEY. With Illustrations. 1 vol., 12mo. $2.00.

"Miss Buckley, the friend of Sir Charles Lyell, and for many years the secretary of the great geologist, in this volume has given a continuous, methodical, and complete sketch of the main discoveries of science from the time of Thales, one of the seven wise men, B. C. 700, down to the present day. The work is unique in its way, being the first attempt ever made to produce a brief and simple history of science. The author has entirely succeeded in her labors, evincing judgment, learning, and literary skill."—*Episcopal Register.*

A Hand-Book of Architectural Styles. Translated from the German by W. COTLETT-SANDERS. 1 vol., 8vo. With 639 Illustrations. $6.00.

"There is a great amount of information in the book, in a small compass. For one who simply wishes to gain a full knowledge of the various styles of architecture, written in a clear and interesting manner, the volume has not its equal nor rival in the English language. This knowledge will be facilitated by the profuse illustrations, of which there are not less than six hundred and thirty-nine, nearly all handsome specimens of engraving, among which figure a large number of famous buildings, ancient and modern."—*Evening Mail.*

D. APPLETON & CO., 549 & 551 Broadway, N. Y.

THE POPULAR SCIENCE MONTHLY.

CONDUCTED BY

E. L. YOUMANS.

---

*This periodical was started (in 1872) to promote the diffusion of valuable sci-
entific knowledge, in a readable and attractive form, among all classes
of the community, and has thus far met a want supplied by
no other magazine in the United States.*

Eight volumes have now appeared, which are filled with instructive and interesting articles and abstracts of articles, original, selected, translated, and illustrated, from the pens of the leading scientific men of different countries. Accounts of important scientific discoveries, the application of science to the practical arts, and the latest views put forth concerning natural phenomena, have been given by *savants* of the highest authority. Prominent attention has been also devoted to those various sciences which help to a better understanding of the nature of man, to the bearings of science upon the questions of society and government, to scientific education, and to the conflicts which spring from the progressive nature of scientific knowledge.

THE POPULAR SCIENCE MONTHLY has long since ceased to be an experiment. It has passed into a circulation far beyond the most sanguine hopes at first entertained, and the cordial and intelligent approval which it has everywhere met, shows that its close and instructive discussions have been well appreciated by the reading portion of the American people. It has not been its policy to make boastful promises of great things to be done in the future, but rather to appeal to what it has already accomplished as giving it a claim upon popular patronage. But no pains will be spared to improve it and make it still more worthy of liberal support, and still more a necessity to the cultivated classes of the country.

THE POPULAR SCIENCE MONTHLY is published in a large octavo, handsomely printed on clear type, and, when the subjects admit, fully illustrated. Each number contains 128 pages.

Terms: $5 per Annum, or Fifty Cents per Number.

Postage free to all Subscribers in the United States, from January 1, 1875.

A new volume of THE POPULAR SCIENCE MONTHLY begins with the numbers for May and November each year. Subscriptions may commence from any date. Back numbers supplied.

Now Ready, Vols. I., II., III., IV., V., VI., VII., and VIII., of the Popular Science Monthly, embracing the numbers from 1 to 48 (May, 1872, to April, 1876). 8 vols., 8vo. Cloth, $3.50 per vol. Half Morocco, $6.50 per vol.

For Sale, Binding Cases for Vols. I., II., III., IV., V., VI., VII., and VIII., of The Popular Science Monthly. These covers are prepared expressly for binding the volumes of THE POPULAR SCIENCE MONTHLY as they appear, and will be sent to Subscribers on receipt of price. Any binder can attach the covers at a trifling expense. Price, 50 cents each.

ADDRESS   *D. APPLETON & CO., Publishers,*

549 & 551 Broadway, New York.